Creative Play
for your baby

Creative Play
for your baby

Steiner Waldorf expertise
and toy projects for
3 months–2 years

Christopher Clouder and Janni Nicol

An Hachette Livre UK Company

First published in Great Britain in 2007 by Gaia,
a division of Octopus Publishing Group Ltd
2–4 Heron Quays, London E14 4JP

Distributed in the United States and Canada by
Sterling Publishing Co., Inc.,
387 Park Avenue South,
New York, NY 10016–8810

ISBN-13: 978-1-85675-271-8

ISBN-10: 1-85675-271-2

A CIP catalogue record for this book is available from the British Library.

Printed and bound in China

10 9 8 7 6 5 4 3 2 1

Safety notes

The toys in this book have been designed for play with babies up to two
years of age and should be made with due care and attention. All yarn
should be of the kind that does not shed fibres and, when used for hair,
must be stitched on well and tied tightly. All wood must be seasoned
before use (by air- or kiln-drying the cut wood) to avoid cracking and
splitting. Rough or sharp edges on wooden toys must be sanded smooth.
If finishing wood with an oil, use one that will cause no harm if put in
the mouth, such as boiled linseed oil or olive oil. Check toys periodically
for general wear and tear, particularly those with loose or small parts.

Disclaimer

The publisher cannot accept any legal responsibility or liability for
accidents or damage arising from the use of any items mentioned in this
book or in the carrying out of any of the projects.

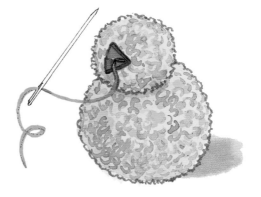

Contents

Introduction 6

Care 12

Awareness 50

Action 72

Wonder 106

Index 126

Further reading 128

Acknowledgements 128

Introduction

Play is joy. When we play, we are fully integrated into ourselves and we feel at one with the world. This is the wisdom of childhood. It does not have to be taught and yet, in order to bear fruit later in life, it needs to be sustained and appreciated. For a young child, the adult's role is that of a protective facilitator and through that activity one finds a childhood in oneself that is both health giving and life enhancing.

Why play matters

For babies, the early years of life are about play. As William Blake put it in his poem 'Infant Joy':

> *"I have no name;*
> *I am but two days old."*
> *What shall I call thee?*
> *"I happy am,*
> *Joy is my name."*
> *Sweet joy befall thee!'*

Play is a wholly absorbing activity from which logic, social skills, memory, fulfilment and values are derived. It is not a negligible aspect of human development, to be relegated to a leisurely pursuit, but in fact lies at the root of our nature. Play encompasses humour, art, bodily wellbeing, human relationships, awareness of one's environment and a sense of self. It is an indication of mental health. The longer we play, the better we learn.

Children can be seen to play better and more deeply when they are nurtured in a loving, secure environment, and what they experience during this time affects their individuality for the rest of their lives. When we debate topical social issues, such as tolerance, citizenship, respect, peace, conflict and ethnic or ideological divisions, we should not forget how our own childhood experiences have contributed to the societies in which we live, with all their varying strengths and weaknesses. Perhaps we should add to the formulation *Homo sapiens* (literally wise man) also *Homo narans*, to designate our need for narrative, and *Homo ludens*, to acknowledge our need for play and laughter, as intrinsic elements of our lives.

Babies are acutely aware of sound. Within hours of birth they can discriminate between human speech and other sounds. They attentively attend to all human activity around them, especially eye contact and facial expressions. A young child pointing at an object is more interested in your reaction to what she is showing than in the object itself – an action that undermines the strange notion that babies are, at heart, egocentric. She is interested in your reaction and already has an 'inter-subjective' mindset, which no other young creature has. She is learning from you what it means to be human and setting up patterns of reaction and interest that will underpin her own character. If you are insensitive or unresponsive,

your reaction is absorbed by her and her incipient
joy of life is rebuked. Your baby wants your time, an
exchange of voices, caring interactions, movement
and feeling. The question of who she is, is answered
by who you are, and playing is fundamental to this.

What is play?

As with the question 'what is love?' or 'what is
peace?', we can define play in a number of ways.
Eventually, however, all answers to the question

prove unsatisfactory because the definitions that
we end up using leave something out that cannot
be described in words. Tangible play contains
intangible qualities. We can recognize play but we
have to be in it to understand and feel what it is;
when we step back from play and only objectify it
we loose that essence. We are dealing with
ambiguity and mystery as well as a purposeful
pursuit. So we must respect what nature has given
us and be prepared to live in this tension, where

we cannot deduce immediate benefit like some mathematical formula or business deal. But we can also smile at our own incompleteness: being a person is never finished and babies can remind us of this infinite potential for growth because they have it in such abundance.

Play is natural. We spend a good proportion of our lives in play. Film, theatre, novels, sports, poetry, music – they all contain qualities of play, and life would be immeasurably poorer without them. We could probably survive their loss but how human would we then be? In all these activities we can transcend ourselves and find a new dimension of existence through our feelings. A baby makes initial contact with the world through play and that becomes a lifetime habit and approach to future challenges. Play is for learning and creativity, but it is also for itself and that is what makes it so difficult to define.

Play is also simple. For a young child, simplicity and repetition are the bedrocks of social interaction. It is endlessly fascinating to watch an adult pick up what you have dropped on the ground from your highchair. A young child loves to hear the same stories and songs. Being alive is novelty enough. She absorbs all gestures, sounds, reactions and

moods and seeks a one-to-one loving relationship with the greatest intensity. There are many arguments for a utilitarian and developmental approach to play and they all have their validity. Play does have an effect on cognitive, social and emotional development but there is also more to it than that.

Play is an expression of the human spirit and shows itself directly and clearly in the child. As well as telling us where we are going, it also tells us where we are coming from. The one-time concept of the child as a blank slate on which upbringing and education could write a recipe for the growing individual is no longer tenable. Nowadays, 'genetic inheritance' implies a mere tendency rather than something that forms individuality through biological determinism. Our children are all unique and they come to us with purpose and character. Play is what reveals that personal essence both to us and to them. Children want to be born and they want the adults that brought them here to be their loving co-discoverers of the world.

Achieving a balanced approach

A baby has forces of life in abundance but needs adults to help balance them so they become integrated into the incipient personality and can be used to serve whatever this newly arrived person wishes to do with her future life. Play does this creatively and with mutual respect. Colour, gesture, sound, expression, tone and quality of material are all part of an introduction to life and so should be a continuation of the positive emotional welcome you give your child. A young child absorbs more than we often realize through the senses and play enables these senses to become stronger in a healthy manner and that, in itself, has a lifelong influence. The young child has limitless imitative competencies and these are an expression of a profound desire to learn. The great learning steps of walking and talking are not solely physical attributes that a child picks up naturally, but key to

The joy of parenting

Many of the world's religions ponder our eventual destiny and what comes after this earthly life. When a baby arrives, it is a propitious time to consider what comes to us in this world. The joy of new parenthood is not just something that arises through a sense of achievement, but is also brought to us by the baby, as a gift. Every baby brings love to her environment as a tangible quality and a reaffirmation that love – or its absence – sits at the core of our relationships.

Watch how people approach your newborn baby and you will notice that they radiate warmth and a benign quality. They will smile, conduct themselves with fewer inhibitions, exude gentleness and exhibit a lightness of being. This is the baby's doing and to respect it we have to put aside our adult assumptions and be prepared to enter a realm we have forgotten. Our years of education and experience can be a barrier that forecloses the simple joys of life that are able to rejuvenate and refresh us. Your baby can overcome those adult limitations for you if you give yourself to the interaction of play. We are then working with human spirit in motion. No one moment is like another and they are all precious.

her relationship to the cosmos and her relationship to fellow human beings. It is also increasingly recognized that bodily movement in a young child is a foundation for later intellectual learning. The wisdom of childhood is that we are integrated, and separating one attribute from another for the purpose of analysis can cause us to lose this vision of ourselves. We shall be exploring these questions throughout the book.

Helping your child

William Blake in his poem 'Infant Sorrow', written as a counterbalance to 'Infant Joy' (see page 6), described a different welcome altogether that a newborn child might experience in the world and the effects that might be produced on the child's subsequent development:

> 'My mother groan'd, my father wept;
> Into the dangerous world I leapt,
> Helpless, naked, piping loud,
> Like a fiend hid in a cloud.'

The child has arrived as a burden and is acutely aware of it. She does not have to be told, she knows. This is a reality for too many children in our world and children for whom childhood is abused or curtailed actually need even more play and its associated ethos of care. Numerous psychological studies have shown that how we welcome children into our families is vitally important for their future development, and we should be prepared to give time and devotion to this task if we wish to have any measure of success as parents. Children need their parents to talk, sing and play with them as they always have done. This represents basic common sense and sensitivity towards the needs of the child.

There is a current trend towards 'kid-pushing', in which the child becomes an early competitive unit whose learning is accelerated in order to keep up with others in the 'real world'. This is based on faulty science and media hysteria and can actually be to the child's detriment by nurturing a premature sense of failure. A baby's brain does not need extra stimulation, as the currently prevailing reductionist view of human nature suggests. A simple game, song or story leaves open and

strengthens the capacities for imagination, creativity, empathy, wonder and fun that are far more important for the growing child as a foundation for future lifelong learning.

Parenting today

Parenting is not an easy undertaking in this frantic, driven and turbulent world. Nevertheless, it does have its own rewards. The following pages show how play can become a meaningful activity for all concerned. In being creative you put something of yourself into the toys and this strengthens your relationship with your child. You should also treat your creations with respect and not discard them unfeelingly or unwittingly because, for your child, they have an emotional reality. She knows what feelings and thoughts you have put into making them and, for her, they are palpable tokens of your care. This in turn helps her awareness to grow in harmony and balance, and her activities to accord with her development. It enables you to share a sense of wonder mutually between you.

This book is for your enjoyment as well as for that of your baby. You will find your baby has much to teach you that can enrich your life if you are prepared to be open to it. Play is risky in that we reveal ourselves and, for an adult, this does not come easily because of our self-consciousness. However, in taking that risk we can discover trusting relationships, akin to those that our children have with the world around them. Playing with your baby is a reciprocal activity, for being a parent is as much about learning as being a child is about growing up.

Steiner Waldorf education

Steiner Waldorf education initially developed at the beginning of the 19th century through the insights of the Austrian philosopher Rudolf Steiner (1861–1925). With origins in the first Waldorf school in Stuttgart in 1919, it is now practised in more

than 950 schools and 1,500 early years settings throughout the world. Its ideas and methods are becoming increasingly influential in mainstream education and in caring for young and school-age children. It works on the basic premise that there are moments in childhood development when there is a propensity to learn in a certain way, and that these specific stages are universally human. As well as the common biological development seen in all children, there is also a more spiritual, inner one, with both general and individual traits. The methodology is, therefore, to teach children in an age-appropriate and health-giving way, and this calls for insight into human nature, creativity and respect for the child.

This way of teaching and learning has a relevance to parents of babies and very young children, as this book demonstrates. The child is central to this form of upbringing and one can learn much through interaction with the child. There is an inherent wisdom in childhood that benefits the parent or teacher not only in being better able to assist the child in growing up as a healthy, active, upright and engaged participant in the modern world, but also in continuing to

develop inwardly oneself. This ensures that the parent-to-child relationship is a creative and fulfilling one, with lasting beneficial effects. Parenting is a long-term vocation and we will not see the results of our input for many years to come. We should not try to create children in our own image, as their future tasks are hidden from us, but we can give them self-esteem, self-knowledge and the wherewithal to develop their own unique capabilities. Here play and playfulness have key roles both in the home and in the classroom.

The first three years of a child's life are bound up with assimilation: she absorbs everything you do or think. So, bringing that child up has a great deal to do with your values and ideals. These are not only explicit in your actions but also implicit in your behaviour towards others and the world. We need to be fully conscious of this, if we hope to attain a better world, in order to become the parents or teachers our children deserve. Steiner education encourages this attitude to life, not as an article of faith, but as a philosophical approach, while showing that everybody has an inborn capacity to act in this way, if given the right understanding and supportive surroundings.

Care

Care

A child brought up in the complete absence of adults would never be able to achieve the full potential of a human being. Those children who are raised in isolation in their first few years, and who thereby miss out on early relationships with others, cannot fully recover such experiences, even if given much care and attention when they are older.

A secure family life

From the first hours after birth a child immerses himself in his relationships with those around him, especially his mother. This powerful motivation is a continuation of the child's spiritual pre-birth experience, in which there was a will to be born on this earth and a wish to be morally effective there. Love plays an essential role in this vital time, with potential long-term effects. Recent studies have shown that a significant proportion of those who, in their own opinion, did not have close relationships with their mothers, experienced mental-health problems later in life. It seems that the love that surrounds us in our first years is irreplaceable.

A child needs to be loved for what he is. The time and space given to a child to experience this quality of care and attention have biological as well as emotional ramifications: they have a real effect on the formation of the brain and conceivably other organs, too. To thrive physically and spiritually, a child needs the security of knowing that you are attentive to his needs and that you can find ways of satisfying them.

Care, therefore, is about creating a secure family life for your baby. The definition of 'family' may differ from culture to culture or even change in certain circumstances, but a young child needs a constant adult factor in his life – one that provides a warm and intimate relationship on which he can wholly rely. From here, he can develop his own perspectives and insights into life. In other words, he grows healthily through what you give him physically, emotionally and spiritually.

Creating balance

A baby does not have the ability to balance his emotions and is therefore dependent on the adult to do this for him until such time as he develops that capacity for himself. Anxiety, stress, fear and emotional deprivation work down into the body and personality of the child and will influence how he deals with such occurrences in the future. If you are conscious of your own feelings and respond to them sensitively, your baby will learn to assimilate his feelings more harmoniously. Our sense of balance – which is both physiological and emotional – allows us to face new situations in life and calmly deal with challenges and potentially difficult circumstances. Living within a secure environment where there is balance through devotion and care at the most vulnerable time of his life enables a child inwardly to develop that

'We are people because of other people.'

African saying

faculty for himself. A caring and sensitive foundation is the birthright of every child and, in becoming a parent, that responsibility is yours.

Absorption and imitation

Care means giving time and adjusting yourself to the needs of your children. In doing so you support them in developing into caring parents themselves: what appears to be your role for the present has repercussions for generations to come. When playing with your child you need to give yourself entirely to it. He needs to see your full attention in what you are doing together.

Your child senses what is going on around him and mirrors what he sees. He is born with a propensity to identify with others and has an inbuilt capacity to be effortlessly emotionally

moved by them. From the very first hours he has an awareness of facial expressions and within two days he will start to change his own facial expression according to what he observes in yours. A parental smile or a frown has a deep impact, therefore. As your child's senses develop so this ability encompasses an ever-wider environment. He is acutely sensitive and imitates both inwardly and outwardly what is presented to him. He is fully engaged in what you are doing, how you move, how you sound and your moods. Everything he observes, including your everyday tasks, provides a basis for his own thought and judgement as he grows towards his individual independence of action and self-fulfilment. A young child not only perceives and imitates our physical actions, but also our moral gestures and thought processes. Referred to as imitation or immersion, what your child is seeking is the oneness he felt before birth.

In *The Education of the Child*, Rudolf Steiner pinpoints how important a child's environment is to his physical and emotional development:

> *'Children learn not by being taught but by imitating. Their physical organs take shape under the influence of their physical surroundings. Healthy vision develops when we ensure that the right colours and lighting is present in the child's surroundings. Similarly, the physical basis of a healthy moral sense develops in the brain and circularity system when children see morality around them.'*

Care through play

Play has a particularly important role in your child's development. He has already exercised play in the womb by moving his legs or sucking his fingers. These actions reflect a pure joy in movement and your child expects this happiness to continue once he is born.

You do not necessarily need to lead the play as an adult, but can allow it to become an activity that you create together. For the baby himself, play is initially social and then, as the months pass, it becomes kinetically, linguistically and spiritually productive. It has nothing to do with training or exercising, but is an expression of human togetherness. As an adult your task is to be an example, to be a partner in play and to provide the materials and the security for play. All three aspects show your caring role. You also have to be aware that your child determines what play is and that this will change. To enjoy play he needs your respect and through imitation he too will learn respect. A child who has been given this level of attention will then have times when he can also play alone. The same feelings of security he experiences when playing with you can be inwardly invoked again: he is still enveloped in your care.

Repetition and role play

Familiarity strengthens self-esteem and what might seem over-repetitive to adults is nourishing for a young child, hence his strong desire for repetitive

When play becomes too much

When playing with your child is fully emotionally involved, the activity itself is important, not simply the end result. However, a child's attention span is limited and requires sensitive handling. There are times when a child needs to turn away. This is not a form of rejection, but rather a healthy inner balancing that should be respected. Early playing is social playing and children need to withdraw at various intervals, just as adults do, in order to become fully engaged again with healthy intensity.

songs, rhymes, phraseology and games: they set a tone of reassurance. Play is also about taking roles and as your child grows he can begin to see that others have perspectives too and can then empathize with them. Through play with you, your child can learn how to differentiate his own experiences and perspectives from those of other people. To feel confident about himself he also needs to be able imaginatively to inhabit others.

Animals, puppets and dolls are all toys that will help develop your child's own nurturing instincts, for he will imitate your behaviour towards him, becoming the carer during play. The simplicity of the toys that feature in this section makes them open-ended, unique and 'living' for your child. They take on a new significance when made by you with effort and patience, themselves becoming objects of warmth created specifically for him. Give thought to the materials you use in the making of these toys, and think of the trees, plants, soil and animals as your child's introduction to nature and all its bounty and beauty.

It is important to appreciate when a child is pushed too far or too little and to act accordingly. By being attentive to your baby's gestures and facial expressions you can respond to his needs. Caring, as an adult, is both a natural and moral inclination, and the sensitivity you show will become the foundation for your child's eventual sensitivity to others.

Simple doll

The doll has always had a special place in childhood. A doll that appeals to a very young child is a doll that feels good to the touch, a doll she can stroke and cuddle. Above all, it is a doll that enables her to imitate the care she receives within her family. Caring for a doll is a natural response from a child who has experienced care herself in warm family relationships.

From three months on, the perfect doll for your baby is a simple one that you have made yourself with loving care. It will have a special value for your child because you have put something of yourself into the making. Even for this age group, it is important to treat a doll with the same respect and loving care that you would show your own child.

Use natural materials that are pleasurable to touch, such as silk, muslin and cotton. These need to be washable, as young babies tend to put toys in their mouths. Do not force a doll on your baby, but wait until she reaches out for it herself. The paediatrician Emmi Pikler, who worked with babies in Hungary from the 1930s to the 1970s, said that it is best to 'listen' to the baby's needs: 'Help me by letting me make my steps by myself.'

A FIRST DOLL

A knotted doll is the simplest you can make, and you may find that your baby will become attached to it in the same way that she does a comforter. It is something she can carry around with her wherever she goes, and may even suck on (which is why hair should be avoided or very firmly attached). There is no need to make a doll with complicated features, clothes or hair. Keep it as simple as possible – it is only later that your baby will begin to recognize the 'human qualities' in her doll, and begin to play with it out of imitation.

Hints and tips
- Keep the doll's features as simple as possible, or leave them out altogether.
- Make sure all the stuffing is tucked into the head, so that your baby cannot chew it.
- If adding simple hair, sew it on well and use yarn that does not leave fibres behind.
- Choose washable fabrics and avoid synthetic materials or those that shrink.
- Use fabric colours that reflect ethnic diversity.
- Make sure cottons are well knotted and finished to leave no loose ends.

'Through the doll the child finds its own self.'

Heidi Britz-Crecelius, *Children at Play*

Making a simple doll

You can make this doll quickly and easily from a square of soft, huggable fabric, such as flannel, towelling or silk. Bear in mind that it will need frequent washing!

How to do it

You will need

Soft fabric

Dressmaking scissors

Carded, unspun sheep's wool *

Thread or yarn

Needle and embroidery thread or coloured pens

Hair-coloured yarn (optional)

Colourful fabric (optional)

*Tease unspun sheep's wool before use, pulling gently to separate dense fibres. A comb-like hand 'carder' speeds up the process.

1 Cut the soft fabric into a square. Experiment with different sizes, depending on the size of doll you want. Choose a small doll for a baby and a larger one for a toddler. Fold the square in half, diagonally, to form a triangle.

2 Find the centre of the folded edge, bunch up the fabric and stuff it with unspun wool to make the doll's head. Secure the neck firmly with thread or yarn.

3 Decide which side is the face and smooth any folds to the back of the head. Sew, or draw, on any features, keeping them simple and expressionless.

4 Form hands by knotting each end of the folded edge, or tie them with thread or yarn. If adding hair, sew the yarn on now.

5 Add clothes if you wish, made from coloured fabric. Try tying a headscarf around the head or wrapping the doll in a blanket.

Cuddly doll

Both boys and girls need to re-enact the care they are given, and doll play will contribute to your child's development into a loving parent. As he grows, the child will involve the doll in his first imaginative play. The simpler the doll, the more scope there is for your child to use his imagination in imitating the care that you give him.

A LIVING DOLL

A more formed doll allows a child to treat it more like a version of himself. He can dress the doll, carry it around like a baby, put it in a hammock to sleep or to feed it. He may treat his doll as a friend, play out his frustrations on it or care for it like a baby. Children begin to recognize human qualities in a doll and it becomes real to them: girls often imitate a mother's actions – playing a mother-and-child game – while boys tend to make the doll into a second self. It is particularly important during this stage to be sensitive as to how you treat your baby's doll. Do not throw it carelessly into the toy box, but respectfully acknowledge that this doll is 'living' for your child.

When making a cuddly doll, keep the features simple. Eyes and mouth are essential, but give them a neutral expression so that the child can imagine the entire range of human emotions when

playing. Just add a small wooden spoon, a bowl and a shawl to wrap the doll in, and play will begin. If you treat this doll as you would your own baby, you will be amazed at the feelings of tenderness and care you will arouse in your child.

Hints and tips
- Keep the doll's features as simple as possible.
- If adding simple hair, sew it on well and use yarn that does not leave fibres behind.
- Choose soft, washable fabric – towelling, flannel or silk – as it will need frequent washing.
- Avoid synthetic materials.
- If you want to add clothes or hats, keep the colours plain and avoid bright patterns.
- Use fabric colours that reflect ethnic diversity.

'A doll is an image of a human being and is therefore suited to develop and enliven the self-image of the growing child.'

Freya Jaffke, *Toymaking with Children*

Making a cuddly doll

The measurements given in the instructions can be adjusted to suit the material you have available (and create dolls of different sizes), but keep them in proportion.

You will need

Carded, unspun sheep's wool *

Thread or yarn

White cotton-knit fabric

Dressmaking scissors

Needle and strong thread

Skin-coloured cotton-knit fabric

Embroidery needle

Red and blue embroidery thread

Tracing paper

Pencil

Single-coloured woollen fabric for arms and legs

Coloured yarn for hair

* Tease unspun sheep's wool before use, pulling gently to separate dense fibres. A comb-like hand 'carder' speeds up the process.

How to do it

1 Make a firm head for the doll using unspun wool to form a tight ball, approximately 9 cm (3½ in) in height. Wrap the ball in a rough square of unspun wool and tie off the excess with thread or yarn. Leave some excess wool as it will give stability to the neck.

2 Wrap the head in a square of white cotton-knit fabric and tie with thread or yarn, again leaving any excess.

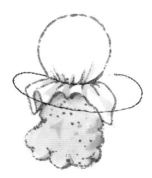

3 Decide which side of the head is to be the face and smooth any folds to the back, binding the head with strong thread at the back and stitching in place.

4 Wrap the head tightly in skin-coloured cotton-knit fabric, with the grain of the fabric running vertically up and down the face. Overlap the edges at the back of the head, turn under the raw edge and sew a vertical seam. Tie off the neck with strong thread and stitch in place.

5 Pull the top edge of the skin-coloured fabric to the back of the head, turn under the raw edges and stitch neatly to secure.

6 Sew on the facial features, keeping the expression simple, and using blue and red embroidery thread for the eyes and mouth. Sew through the head, from the front to the side to make each stitch.

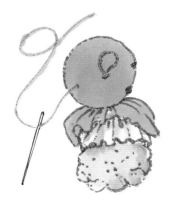

7 Cut a piece of fabric for the arms, about 24 cm (9½ in) × 16 cm (6½ in). Fold in half lengthways, with right sides together. Cut a shallow hole for the neck in the folded edge, as shown in the illustration. Stitch the sleeve seams as shown and turn right side out.

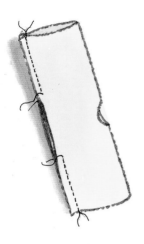

8 Cut another piece of the same fabric for the legs, measuring approximately 30 cm (12 in) × 22 cm (8½ in). Fold in half widthways, with right sides together, and sew a seam along the long edge to create a tube shape.

9 Re-fold the fabric tube, so that the seam now forms the back seam. Draw the inner leg outline on to the fabric and sew as one continuous seam, as shown in the illustration. Snip out the material between the legs, close to the seams.

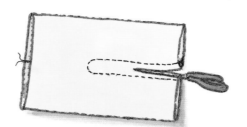

10 Fold each leg, as if for ironing a crease down the centre, and sew the foot seam running from front to back, curving it gently towards the heel. Trim any excess fabric and turn the legs right side out.

11 Assemble the doll. Tuck the neck end of the head through the hole in the folded edge of the arm section and stitch to the neck to hold. Make a small bag from excess fabric and stuff it firmly with wool. This will form a stuffed core, or stomach, for the doll. Sew it firmly to the neck end of the head.

12 Stuff the leg section lightly and run a few gathering stitches around the waist. Attach the legs to the stuffed body, pulling the gathered waist over the stomach. Draw on the threads until tight and stitch the leg section to the stomach.

13 Stuff the arm section lightly, then pull the fabric down to meet the trouser section at the waist. Turn under the raw edges and stitch in place.

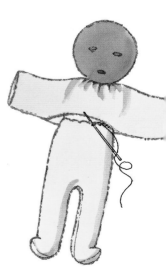

14 Make a hand, using a piece of skin-coloured fabric about 6 cm (2½ in) × 4 cm (1½ in). Fold in half widthways, right sides together, and draw on a simple hand outline like the one shown below. Stitch around the outline, leaving an opening at the wrist for stuffing. Repeat to make the other hand.

15 Turn under the raw edges of the wrists of the arm section, sew a few gathering stitches, draw up the threads and secure. Turn the hands right side out, stuff lightly and stitch to the wrist ends.

16 Sew on yarn for hair, attaching it firmly. Run a few gathering stitches around the ankles of the doll to give the feet shape.

Floor puppets

As your baby becomes more active, and begins to play on the floor, these simple figures will enable her to become more creative in her interaction with others. These are recognizable people with whom your baby can play and identify. They stand firmly, yet are soft enough to pick up gently, and can also be taken to bed, or on an outing, and cuddled.

ROLE PLAY

Try building a small floor scene involving the puppets, then pick up one of the figures and use it to talk to another. You will soon find that, as your baby moves around, she is attracted by your play, and will begin to imitate your actions, picking up another puppet and doing what you do.

Give the puppets names: 'mummy', 'daddy', 'sister' or 'brother' are fine, but if you wish to give them proper names, make sure you use the same one each time you refer to the puppet person. This helps your baby to begin to recognize that names refer to people. When playing with the floor puppet, she can then care for it as if for a real person. The floor puppet becomes real in her play, and you will see that she begins to play out what she sees happening around her.

Whenever you interact with a puppet or doll, remember to make it believable. The baby will soon pick up on your own lack of belief if you overact with the puppet. Gentle conversation and physical care are what your baby will imitate.

FLOOR SCENES

It is easy to build up a floor scene that involves a number of floor puppets. Simply place a piece of coloured cloth on the floor, make a little house by draping a differently coloured cloth over a box, and use fencing or blocks (such as those on page 78) to create boundaries for a garden. For a farm, you could use green or brown cloth for fields and blue cloth for a pond.

You can show how we care for each other, by having a puppet play out everyday activities, such as feeding animals in a farmyard, chicks in a garden or ducks on a pond. Your child will begin to imitate your play and her imagination will soon become active. She will place a puppet next to the animals in the scene, to 'look after' them. Take a puppet with you on an outing to the park, so that the puppet can watch your baby feed the ducks – then the puppet will know how to do it too!

Hints and tips
- Make a family of puppets, beginning with mother and father.
- Use plain colours and strong fabric – felt is ideal because it does not fray.
- Sew heads firmly to their bodies.
- Making a cardboard disc for the base helps the puppet to stand solidly.
- Use different skin colours to reflect a range of cultures.
- Sew hair, scarf and clothes on securely.

Making a floor puppet

Use this project to make a range of puppets of different sizes. You can make the measurements larger or smaller, but keep them in roughly the same proportions to each other.

How to do it

You will need

Carded, unspun sheep's wool *

Thread or yarn

Sharp scissors

Skin-coloured cotton-knit fabric

Needle and thread

Embroidery needle

Embroidery threads to match skin and hair colours

Pins (optional)

Coloured felt

Thin card

Hair-coloured carded, unspun sheep's wool

Colourful fabric (optional)

*Tease unspun sheep's wool before use, pulling gently to separate dense fibres. A comb-like hand 'carder' speeds up the process.

1 Make a firm head for the doll using unspun sheep's wool to form a tight ball, approximately 4 cm (1½ in) in height. Wrap the ball in a rough square of unspun wool and tie off the excess with thread or yarn. Leave some excess wool as it will give stability to the neck.

2 Wrap the head tightly in a square of skin-coloured cotton-knit fabric, with the grain of the fabric running vertically up and down the face. Overlap the edges at the back of the head, turn under the raw edge and sew a vertical seam.

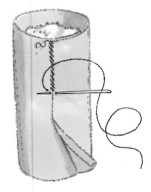

3 Pull the top edge of the cotton-knit fabric to the back of the head, turn under the raw edges and stitch them neatly. Tie a length of thread around the base of the head to form the neck.

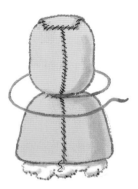

4 Stitch on the facial features, keeping them simple. Use pins to act as guides for positioning, if desired.

5 Make the body. Cut a piece of felt about 9 x 14 cm (3½ x 5½ in) and join the short edges to make a cylinder. Turn the cylinder inside out, so the seam is on the inside. Cut a small card disc to fit in the base of the cylinder and a slightly larger felt disc for finishing off the body (see Step 7).

6 Fold in the top edge of the felt cylinder and make a row of gathering stitches. Gather, and sew the cylinder to the head.

7 Stuff the felt body with wool, without packing too firmly. Insert the small card disc and place the felt disc over the top, stitching it neatly to the base of the felt cylinder.

8 Stitch a tuft of unspun sheep's wool on to the doll's head for hair.

9 Add additional clothes if you wish to dress the puppet, making them from coloured fabric.

Wall hanging

Instead of giving a baby a doll's house, which is much more the domain of a five- to six-year-old, you can use this wall hanging as a place for your child to house her toys. Everything will have its place, and there is nothing that a baby loves more than putting something away . . . and taking it out again.

IMITATIVE PLAY

All parents want their children to learn to tidy away their toys. Clearing up should follow playtime as logically as waking follows sleep. Caring for your baby's toys by finding them a home and putting them away properly will convey that what you have made for your child is worth caring for, and that everything should be treated with the love and respect it deserves. Children are pleased by order, and giving everything its right place also makes them feel secure.

You will soon begin to see that your baby imitates your behaviour, finding the perfect pocket for each of the toys that you can make using this book. Standing puppet figures will go into a 'house' pocket, the ducks into a 'pond', animals into a 'pen', and so on. Your baby won't be able to find the correct pockets immediately, for it is not yet time for recognition of abstract symbols. This comes with familiarity with a real duck on a pond, or with the sudden awareness of the child's own house. You can help by putting things away with your baby, referring to the pockets by name so that each toy has its home. Soon your baby's imagination will set to work and the wall hanging will not simply be a storage unit, but also a plaything.

PLAY THROUGH SONG

You can easily make up a tune for a 'tidying up' song, using simple words and a sing-song voice. You can sing the same song for any tidying situation. Singing the song even before you begin to tidy will act as a signal to your baby that it's time to clear the toys away:

'Tidy time, it's tidy time,
Time to tidy up today, time to put it all away,
It's tidy time, it's tidy time.'

Hints and tips

- Keep the design simple.
- Use strong backing material.
- Sew on the pockets well, making each big enough to store toys in.
- Start by making only a few pockets.
- Make each pocket recognizable: a duck pond for a duck, a pen for a lamb.
- Use your imagination to decorate the pockets, but keep it simple.
- Position the wall hanging so that it is low enough for your baby to reach – from a doorknob or in the cot, for example.
- Secure the wall hanging well so that it cannot be pulled down.
- Do not attach the wall hanging to furniture that can be toppled over easily.

Making a wall hanging

Use your imagination when designing the pockets for this project. Choose images and motifs that your baby will recognize, and to reflect what the pockets will contain.

You will need

Thick backing fabric in a single colour

Tape measure

Dressmaking scissors

Needle and threads to match fabric colours

Two garden canes

Tracing paper

Pencil

Coloured felt and fabric

Selection of buttons and beads

PVA glue

Craft knife or saw

Thick yarn

How to do it

1 Cut the sturdy backing fabric to measure approximately 60 x 90 cm (24 x 36 in).

2 Hem the long sides of the wall hanging. Then hem the top and bottom of the hanging, leaving a big enough gap for the garden cane to slide through.

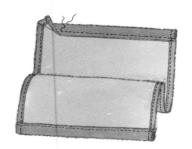

3 Draw your design for the wall hanging on tracing paper: the idea is to make a number of useful, colourful pockets. It helps to lay the tracing paper over the backing fabric to make sure everything fits.

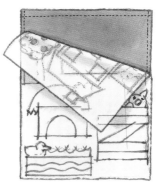

4 Follow your traced design to make up each pocket from a selection of coloured felt and fabric. Make sure the pockets are big enough for toys to fit inside.

5 Sew the pockets on to the backing fabric and sew or glue on any additional decorations.

6 Use a craft knife or saw to cut each garden cane to width, adding 2 cm (1 in) at each end so that it overhangs the fabric.

7 Use a craft knife to score a groove approximately 1 cm (½ in) in from each end of the top cane before threading both canes through the wall hanging.

8 Make a loop for hanging the finished piece. You can finger knit, crotchet or plait thick yarn. The finished length needs to be about 100 cm (39 in).

9 Attach the loop to the top cane, tying it on where you made the grooves, and glue to secure if desired.

Doll's hammock

Rocking, for all of us, is comforting, nurturing and reassuring. Rocking a simple or cuddly doll (see pages 18 and 21) is pleasurable for a child too. By making a hammock to rock the doll in, you enable your child to 'put the doll to bed' in the most unusual places, as part of her play.

APPROPRIATE CARE

You can hang the hammock between chairs, from table leg to bookshelf or across your baby's cot, and you can take it out into the garden, on holiday or to the seaside. Bringing the hammock into different environments will begin to initiate the play of which all small children are capable. Your child can use the hammock as a rucksack or basket to carry the doll around in, for example – there are many possibilities for modifications.

When you are introducing your child to the hammock and its possibilities, care for the doll as you would your own baby. Add a simple plain blanket to wrap the doll in. You can cut this from old cloth, or knit it, but be sure to finish it by edging it nicely, as you would everything you make for your baby.

When you place the doll in the hammock, wrap it in the blanket, tuck it in carefully and then sing a lullaby, such as the old nursery rhyme:

'Rock-a-bye baby on the treetop
When the wind blows, the cradle will rock
When the bough breaks, the cradle will fall
And down will come baby, cradle and all.'

Don't worry about the words of nursery rhymes. Young children don't question them, but are simply lulled by the rhythm of your singing. They will soon be singing it themselves or asking you to sing to them as you put them to bed.

Putting a baby doll to bed is a wonderful way of demonstrating care in all its forms, and if you show your love for the doll, as you do for your own baby, it will make an immense difference to the way your child treats the doll herself. As she grows up, you will see that her caring attitude is expressed in the way she treats other children, too.

Hints and tips

- Hem the hammock fabric well, so that there are no ragged edges.
- Sand the ends of the canes carefully so that there are no rough edges.
- Make the cords by finger-knitting yarn or making a simple rope.
- When hanging the hammock, be sure to secure it to something stable.
- Show how you care for the doll by tucking it in gently with its blanket.
- Rock the hammock softly, singing a lullaby.

Making a doll's hammock

Use a lightweight but strong fabric, such as muslin or cotton. If the canes are not too long, and you gather up the material, you will achieve a deeper, more stable hammock.

How to do it

You will need

Two garden canes

Craft knife or saw

Sandpaper

Muslin cloth

Tape measure

Dressmaking scissors

Needle and thread

Thick yarn

PVA glue (optional)

1 Use the craft knife or saw to cut each garden cane to 40 cm (16 in) in length. Sand the raw edges smooth.

2 Cut a piece of muslin cloth measuring 50 × 80 cm (20 × 32 in). To make a stronger hammock, double either one of the measurements and fold the fabric in half. Sew a hem down each of the long sides.

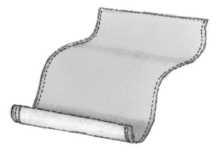

3 Sew a hem along each of the short sides, making it deep enough for a garden cane to pass through.

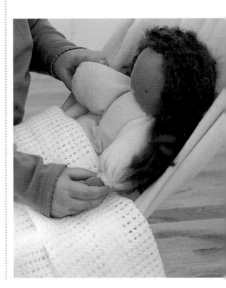

4 Use the craft knife to score a groove approximately 1 cm (½ in) in from the end of each cane before threading the canes through the hammock.

5 Make two loops to be used for hanging the hammock. You can finger knit, crotchet or plait thick yarn. The finished length needs to be about 55–60 cm (21–24 in).

6 Attach a length to each cane, tying it on where you made the grooves. Glue to secure, if desired. The fabric should bunch up a little between the cords.

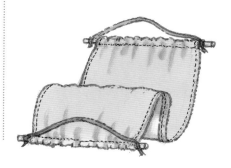

Soft hen

Many children never experience farm life, and it is difficult for them to imagine how animals behave, or even to recognize certain animals, until they have seen them for themselves. You can help by singing rhymes that help your baby to identify with the animal. Around the age of two, a child will appreciate simple, repetitive stories about different animals.

FARMYARD LIFE

This soft hen provides a good introduction to farm animals. Hens and chickens make a lot of noise and the clucking or 'puck, puck, pucking' is a sound that all babies love to imitate. (This can be accompanied by lots of tickling!) In the beginning, your baby will cuddle the soft hen as he would any soft toy. It is too early for him to recognize it as a hen. Naming it 'mummy' hen and giving it a voice to chirp with will begin to give your baby a picture of its difference to the knitted sheep, for example (see page 42).

Hints and tips
- Sew on the comb well to prevent your baby chewing it off.
- Choose a warmly coloured felt for the hen's body, say a rich, golden brown.
- Use the same, or similar, colour for the wings, but avoid using too many different colours.
- Make some smaller chicks in yellow felt so that 'mummy' hen can care for her babies.
- Give the hen a collar when it is going out in the pushchair, so that you can tie it on securely.

THE CONCEPT OF A FAMILY

If you make another hen as a friend, and some baby chicks, mummy hen and auntie can begin to care for the babies. You can make a rooster simply by using a different coloured felt, making a bigger comb for the top of the head, and adding one under the chin. The scenario of a family with adults caring for little ones is something that your baby can relate to, and helps him to feel safe and secure.

One idea is to make a plate of 'food' for the hen and chicks to eat (some spun wool or felt offcuts in a dish made from an open shell, or even some bread crusts). This will give the child an image of the actions that chickens make when feeding, which he can also begin to relate to himself.

Extending play with the hen's family could involve creating a farm scene, with the floor puppets (see page 26) feeding hens and chicks in a simple pen (made with the blocks and fences on page 78). Calling 'dinner time', while putting down the 'food' and gathering the hens and chicks to eat, will create an impression in the child's mind that man and animal come when dinner is called. These games will all also demonstrate that caring for animals is as important as caring for each other.

Making a soft hen

Make this hen small enough for your baby to hold comfortably. The example here is approximately 12 cm (5 in) wide. Stuff it so that it is soft and squishy.

How to do it

You will need

Paper

Pencil

Brown felt

Red felt

Sharp scissors

Embroidery needle

Red and black embroidery thread

Stiff card

Carded, unspun sheep's wool *

* Tease unspun sheep's wool before use, pulling gently to separate dense fibres. A comb-like hand 'carder' speeds up the process.

1 Draw a design for a hen on paper and use as a template to cut the shapes from brown and red felt. You need a simple body shape (twice), two wing shapes and a comb.

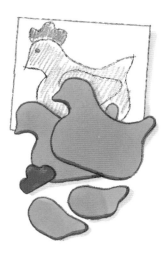

2 Sew a wing on to each body shape, checking that they are roughly in the same position. Use a blanket stitch and red embroidery thread.

3 Sew the two body shapes together, right sides out, using blanket stitch. Sew the red felt comb in position between the two parts, and leave a gap at the tail end of the hen for stuffing.

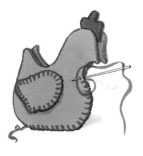

4 Insert a strip of stiff card to flatten the base of the hen slightly for standing and stuff the hen with unspun wool, so that the hen is plump but not firm.

5 Sew up the gap at the tail end. Complete the hen by sewing an eye on each side of the head, using black embroidery thread.

Knitted sheep

A sheep is the first simple, knitted animal that you can make for your baby to play with. There are so many different ways in which he can interact with a simple toy like this. He can cuddle it in his cot, drag it around with him while he is learning to crawl and use it for floor play when he is old enough to begin playing imaginatively.

Children identify with sheep and lambs, possibly because of the many nursery rhymes about these animals that are sung to them. 'Baa Baa Black Sheep' is a particular favourite, especially if you play with your baby's fingers when you are singing it. 'Mary had a Little Lamb' is another popular nursery rhyme, which demonstrates the love between Mary and her lamb. It's worth making the trip to the countryside or a neighbourhood farm to watch the lambs gambolling in the fields during the spring, and all babies will relate to seeing these little creatures being bottle-fed.

Hints and tips
- Use a soft yarn in pure wool, undyed if possible.
- Stuff the sheep carefully to give it the right shape and pose.
- Make sure you sew the sheep up well to prevent the wool stuffing coming out.
- Make the tail from crocheted or twisted yarn.
- Create a family by making a companion dark brown sheep and a number of little white baby lambs.

FEELING SECURE

Lambs, ducks and chicks are a child's first and favourite farm animals. If you enlarge your family of toy animals by making your sheep some little lambs, you will be able to demonstrate how mummy sheep can look after her babies – just as you look after yours. The image of an adult always taking care of little ones is familiar to babies. Yours will see this as a reflection of his own life – not in a conscious way, but in a way that makes him feel deeply secure in his own family relationships. When a baby knows where he is in the world, with a rhythm and loving warmth supporting him, he becomes relaxed and secure.

FLOOR PLAY

When your baby is old enough for floor play, he will enjoy building little scenes with you. You could use soft cloths in different colours for fields and streams, pine cones for trees and a large flat shell for a water trough. To create the farm boundaries, use home-made wooden fences (see page 78). Add floor puppets (see page 26) to be Old MacDonald, his wife and children, and develop scenarios in which they take care of the animals. This will help your baby to develop his imaginative play and he will begin to re-enact what he sees happening in the world around him, including experiences of his own.

Making a knitted sheep

The knitting instructions give different sets of numbers which should be followed consistently for the large, medium or small size of sheep. Mould the sheep into shape as you stuff it.

How to do it

You will need

Natural, undyed yarn

Two 3¼ mm (US 3) knitting needles

Needle and sewing thread

Carded, unspun sheep's wool *

Pencil

Sharp scissors

1 Follow the diagram to knit the body of the sheep using garter stitch (knitting every row). Always use the first, second or third number for a large, medium or small sheep.

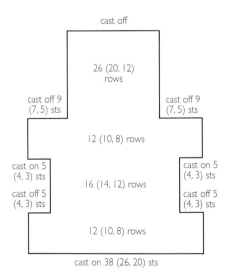

cast off

26 (20, 12) rows

cast off 9 (7, 5) sts

cast off 9 (7, 5) sts

12 (10, 8) rows

cast on 5 (4, 3) sts

cast on 5 (4, 3) sts

16 (14, 12) rows

cast off 5 (4, 3) sts

cast off 5 (4, 3) sts

12 (10, 8) rows

cast on 38 (26, 20) sts

2 To make the largest sheep: cast on 38 stitches; knit 12 rows; cast off 5 stitches at the beginning of the next two rows; knit 16 rows; cast on 5 stitches at the beginning and end of the next row; knit 12 rows; cast off 9 stitches at the beginning of the next two rows; knit 26 rows; cast off.

3 Fold the knitted piece in half, lengthways along the body. Fold each of the legs in half lengthways and stitch into a tube, closing up the foot. As you work, stuff each leg with the unspun sheep's wool. Pack the wool tightly and use a pencil to push it down firmly into the foot.

4 Sew up the sheep's tummy, creating a larger tube. Stuff the sheep through either the head or rear end, moulding it to the required shape as you work. Stuff firmly, but do not pack the body as tightly as the legs. Sew up the rear opening.

* Tease unspun sheep's wool before use, pulling gently to separate dense fibres. A comb-like hand 'carder' speeds up the process.

5 Now make the head. Sew the folded edges together at A, then run some gathering stitches through both layers of fabric between B and C. Pull lightly, to bring the nose end in towards the top of the forelegs and create a head shape. Insert stuffing, then stitch to secure.

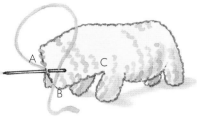

6 Finger knit or plait a yarn tail and sew on.

7 Knit the ears in garter stitch, following the diagram. Use the first set of measurements for the large sheep and the second set for the medium or small sheep. To make the larger ear, cast on 4 stitches; knit 2 rows; cast on 1 stitch at the beginning and end of the next row; knit 5 rows; cast off 1 stitch at the beginning of the next 2 rows; cast off.

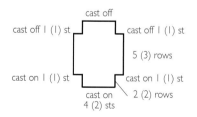

8 Repeat to make a second ear and sew the ears on to either side of the head.

Pompom chick

Pompoms are easy and fun to make (see page 82) and can be used in different sizes to form the basis of a variety of animals, including this pompom chick. Adding a beak and eyes gives the chick identity, although you will find that your baby does not really need detailed additional features for the chick to be recognizable as a chick.

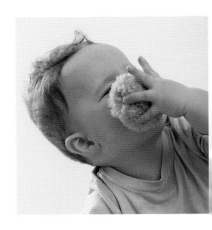

IDENTIFICATION
A chick can be formed of nothing more than a small pompom attached to a larger one, to create the head and body. As long as you introduce a chick with the right actions and chirping noises,

Hints and tips
- Use natural materials – pure wool rather than acrylic yarn, for example.
- Use realistic colours that are not too bright – pale yellow for example.
- Keep the facial features simple and sew them on very securely.
- For hints and tips on making the pompoms, see page 82.

your baby will soon begin to identify with it. Make the chick small enough for your baby to grasp and lift with ease. Children love the soft, cuddly feel of this toy and enjoy holding it to their faces. For this reason, construct it sturdily. If possible, take your baby to see a newborn chick. Children react joyfully to these little bundles of fluff and, when they see how fragile the tiny creatures are, they understand how gently and carefully they must be handled.

IMAGINATIVE PLAY
Do not worry that the farmyard animals you might make for your child, such as the pompom chick, the soft hen (see page 38) and the knitted sheep (see page 42), are all different sizes. This does not make any difference to your baby. Babies are more concerned with the sensory experience and the opportunities toys give for interaction. This is what strengthens imaginative play.

'While watching children play it becomes clear how easily a child imagines himself in the centre of a farmyard with lots of animals.'

Freya Jaffke, *Toymaking with Children*

Making a pompom chick

This simple chick is made from two sizes of pompom. You can vary the colours and decorative details to make all manner of cuddly animals.

How to do it

(see page 84)

1 Follow the steps for making pompoms (see page 84) to make two fluffy yellow balls – a large one for the chick's body and a smaller one for its head.

2 Attach the smaller pompom to the large one. Use a few stitches in a matching thread, making sure you stitch through the centre of the pompom and pull tight to secure.

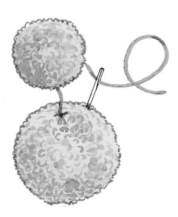

3 Cut a small diamond shape from the orange felt, fold in half to make a beak shape and stitch in place through the fold, using orange thread. Sew deep into the pompom and pull tightly.

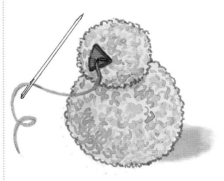

4 Decide where you want to position the eyes and stitch two small brown dots using brown thread.

You will need

Sheet of card

Compass

Pencil

Sharp scissors

Yellow yarn

Needle

Yellow, orange and brown thread

Orange felt

introducing concepts of smooth and rough. A young child needs to feel soft and hard, warm and cold but not to extremes – his introduction to the world through this sense should be a pleasurable one.

Smell, taste, sight and sound are crucial from an early stage of life. A baby has an acute sense of smell and can readily detect where his mother has been. A scent or smell provides a connectedness or an aversion to our environment and a multiplicity of smells adds richness to our lives. That the toys in this book are simple does not imply an avoidance of what appeals to a baby's sense of smell: you can engage your child through the fresh, gentle and natural scents of the materials that you use.

All babies put things in their mouths. The sense and experience of taste are related to what we find attractive and therefore have implications for what we later find aesthetically pleasing in our environment. For this reason, toys should be made with care: comb the hair for dolls, sew in regular stitches, avoid any raggedness and carefully sand rough wooden surfaces. You should care for the appearance of the toys just as you do your child's appearance, so demonstrating that care for oneself is balanced by care for the world and others.

Colour and light are not just physical attributes but have a spiritual dimension as well. Play with colours and, when making toys, use materials that look harmonious together. Early colour experiences help vitalize a child's appreciation of the world: drab, lifeless colours are uninteresting and can be depressing, while those that are too bright or garish are shocking and over-stimulating.

The toys you make need narratives that appeal to your baby's sense of hearing and can offer opportunity for his linguistic ability to develop. Create stories as you play and find words that hone in on what the child himself is being attentive to. Carefully adjust what you say or sing to your baby's capacity to absorb sounds and allow time for him to appreciate the inherent beauty of sounds. Excessive and loud sounds cause a child to turn away and diminish personal connection. The same

The role of movement

One of the first steps towards self-awareness comes through the sense of movement. A baby perceives his own movement and is fascinated by it. For a young child the experience is so impressive that he desires continual repetition as he strives to obtain control of his own body. You can nurture this through purposeful activity and by enticing your child to enjoy his own movements. Do not play *for* the baby, making him into a passive observer, but rather play *with* him so that your responses are consequent to his movements. Playing is not in the first instance a baby pacifier, but baby developer: avoid toys that move electronically because, although they may attract momentary attention, they do not relate to a baby's age-developmental needs and allow no scope for self-directed creative movements.

applies to words: the tone in which you say something also brings nuances of meaning. The gestures with which you accompany your words can reinforce their truthfulness as you speak or move the toys and help the child discover the scale of human emotions in a controlled fashion.

Emotional awareness

Your baby experiences comfort and harmony through everyday life. When all is well – when there is order, rhythm and harmony and things happen when they should – his sense of harmony is enhanced. Overwhelming stress, violent gestures or handling, nervousness and wilfulness in daily life can obstruct the healthy development of this sense. Parents are not superhuman and it is inevitable that our own biography and events in our lives impinge on our relationship with our children. Playing with a child or baby, however, is a way of redressing the balance in ourselves and therefore restoring the harmony: remember, a relationship works both ways. Building some regularity into the times when you play together will work positively on both of you. Create an expected routine and give yourself fully to the play at that time.

Your child needs physical, emotional and spiritual warmth. He loves the toys that you give him, this early attachment being a step towards becoming attached to the world. In play you should treat all toys with respect and your child will feel the loving, warm quality that you have put into making them with him in mind. This loving care is not to be underestimated: warmth and coldness dictate many of our experiences in life and our sense of warmth has great influence on our social attitudes and capacities. Your warmth towards your baby must be genuine, however, as children readily see through any pretence or exaggeration.

Developing self-awareness

The experimental child psychologist Peter Hobson refers to the experience of being a baby and a toddler as 'the cradle of thought'. Through his perceptions, a baby begins to grasp what is right and what is not. The sense of thought awakens as, usually in his second year, he begins to separate his own self from the selves of others, and starts to appreciate his relationship to the world. The narrative train of thought that emerges through playful activity nourishes this sense and these connections develop into meanings. Our thoughts tend to meander and are greatly influenced by our feelings, so being truthful and accurate are essential here. We do not need to teach thoughts to a young child because he can extract them out of his environment himself, but your toys and games can help if they seek to involve the child in social engagement that is typically human.

If your child experiences your loving and positive emotional care, his sense of himself and the 'other', or sense of ego, will be well nurtured. It first comes to expression at about one year of age when his imagination begins to explore his natural and universal awareness of 'inter-subjectivity' with interest and joyfulness. The toys in this section are effective, therefore, because they attract a child's healthy interest through all his senses, are capable of mirroring complex and changing emotional states and are made with the assumption that the world has more depth than the purely materialistic.

Rattles and shakers

Discovering the world, and exploring everything that she comes into contact with, is what occupies your baby when she is awake. It may be her hands and feet, her clothing or the blanket in her cot that fascinates her. When you give her something new, such as a rattle or shaker, the joy and interest are multiplied.

Rattles appeal to the senses of touch, hearing and sight, and also stimulate movement and balance. The feel of the different textures of objects on a rattle will engage your baby and draw her attention. She will enjoy the objects attached, taking an interest in their variety and shape, their texture and sound. This is the start of her ability to recognize a range of different textures.

Hints and tips

- When making ring rattles, secure all items well.
- Do not add too many items: rattles should not be too noisy.
- Keep rattles simple: they should not be too bright or many coloured.
- Your baby is likely to chew a ring rattle, so do not attach anything that can come off in the mouth.
- Use boiled linseed oil or olive oil instead of varnish on wood. Allow it to soak in before rubbing off until the wood shines. This makes it safe for chewing.
- If using a box with a lid for a shaker, make sure that it will not come apart.
- Fill a box shaker only with tiny items that your baby cannot choke on.
- Box shakers must be small enough for little fingers to grasp.
- Tie a rattle or shaker to your baby's pushchair or pram when going out.

DEVELOPMENT OF THE PHYSICAL BODY

If you hold a rattle above your baby and shake it gently, she will respond by stretching out her hand to catch it. This involves the initiation of the will to move – the same force that drives the developing child to sit, stand and walk. She will learn to overcome the involuntary reflex movements over which she has no control and will develop those that she can control out of her own self-direction.

Your baby will take great delight in your playful interaction with her. Her favourite activity once she can sit up will be to throw, drop or bang toys. A wonderful game will take shape: she will shake, bang and then drop the rattle. Each time you pick it up and shake it for her, she will take it from you, laugh with joy – and drop it again. And so the game continues! The repetition is important, as it helps to develop the strength and co-ordination of the physical body.

'The ball is the first toy a child should have, for it is the symbol of the whole.'

Friedrich Froebel

Making a fleece ball

A quicker method for making these balls is to reach the soaking and soaping stage (Step 3), then tie the ball in a stocking and place in a washing machine on a short hot cycle.

How to do it

1 Make a ball from unspun sheep's wool, using thin strands wrapped tightly around each other in a random pattern. Shape them into a ball as you go, making it a third bigger than the intended finished size – it will shrink in the making process.

2 Use coloured yarn for the last layer, again wrapping the strands tightly around the ball in a random fashion.

3 Submerge the ball in a bowl of warm water until it is soaked. Squirt the ball generously with washing-up liquid or rub all over with olive soap.

• Tease unspun sheep's wool before use, pulling gently to separate dense fibres. A comb-like hand 'carder' speeds up the process.

4 Now cup the ball as if making a snowball and 'pack' the surface with a pressing motion. Rub the ball, making sure you continue to keep its round form. Continue to cup and rub the ball in this fashion, working quickly so that the outer fibres begin to lock.

5 You need to work the ball for at least 5–7 minutes for the felting to begin, before rinsing the ball in cold water, still working it as above. This helps to firm the locking of the fibres.

6 Re-submerge the ball in warm water, add more soap if you need to, and work for another 5 minutes.

7 Rinse thoroughly in cold water, squeezing out all of the soap. Rub in a towel and dry.

8 The ball will take a long time to dry out properly – place it on top of a radiator or in the airing cupboard to speed up the process.

Wind chime

Your baby does not need too much to play with in the first few months because his main task is to build physical strength through muscle development. He also needs to recognize and understand his body, and become accustomed to what it is capable of doing. Therefore toys that he can look at while lying in his cot, or when sitting in his highchair or pram outside, will catch his attention, particularly if they make a sound.

EARLY SIGHTS AND SOUNDS

At this age, the protection of the senses is vital. Too much or too loud a noise prevents the hearing from developing sensitively, hindering your baby's ability to differentiate between the sounds he hears. Similarly, too many objects placed around a baby, particularly if they are bright or patterned, can be overpowering, and the baby will not be attracted to them in the same way as he might be if given only one simple toy at a time.

Anything that your baby is able to focus on in the early months needs to be made from simple materials and to be pleasing to the eye. It is not necessary for the baby to be familiar with the objects, as that will come when he begins to experience for himself where these belong in nature. It is what the object does that will interest him – or what he can make it do.

If you hang the wind chime in a place where the wind will catch it, such as in front of an open window during summer, the breeze will make it swing and twirl gently, and the sound of the hollow canes, shells, beads and other dangling ornaments as they move will make soft and sweet music to your baby's ears.

Hints and tips
- Make your wind chime small enough to hang inside and out.
- Make use of natural materials that can be found and used easily: shells have natural holes for threading, for example.
- Use strong string or thread that will not rot if the wind chime is hung outside.
- Sand the wood and bamboo well, so there are no sharp edges.
- Oil wood and bamboo to protect from weathering.
- Keep all parts of the wind chime out of reach of your child.

'The young child is all sense-organ.'

Rudolf Steiner

Making a wind chime

When selecting beads for this wind chime, make sure you choose some pretty coloured-glass ones that will catch the light as the chime twirls in a breeze.

How to do it

You will need

Slice of seasoned log

Vice

Drill and drill bits

Power sander (if removing all bark) or sandpaper

Boiled linseed oil or olive oil and cloths

Bamboo

Coping saw

Strong nylon string

Sharp scissors

Long needle (optional)

Ceramic or glass beads

Shells and stones

Large wooden beads (optional)

1 Place the slice of log, approximately 25 mm (1 in) thick, in a vice. Draw two lines diagonally from corner to corner on a rectangle of paper smaller than your slice of log, marking the corners and the intersection of the two lines. Place the diagram on top of the log and follow it to drill five small holes. You will use these for suspending the wind chime.

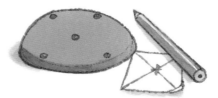

2 With the slice of log still in the vice, use the power sander to remove any bark. (If you don't want to remove the bark completely, you can simply sand off any loose bits by hand.) To protect the wood, oil it and polish with a cloth.

3 Use a coping saw to cut the bamboo to length – you need four roughly equal lengths. As a feature, trim the ends at 30 degrees. Oil and polish the bamboo lengths.

4 Drill two small holes opposite each other at the top of each length of bamboo. Feed a long piece of strong nylon string through the two holes, using a long needle if desired.

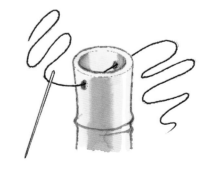

5 Once through the bamboo, tie a knot in the string and thread a bead on. Tie another knot to keep the bead in place. Repeat this before threading the ends of the nylon string through one of the corner holes in the log slice. Tie another knot to secure and add a bead if desired.

6 Repeat Step 5 for the three remaining lengths of bamboo.

7 Make a central string, decorated with colourful beads and/or natural objects, and thread the end of this string through the central hole in the log slice. Secure as described in Step 5.

8 Draw all string ends together above the log slice. You can twist, plait or knot them any way you like to keep them tidy and central to the log slice for suspending. Threading them through large wooden beads is an effective way of doing this.

Flowerpot bells

The warmth of love flowing from you generates a different response in your baby from that when you hold an object out to him. If you give your child a toy, he will play with it for a few minutes, and drop it. If you give him your finger, he will play with it and hold on to it, for it belongs to you. He can feel your love, care and attention and his senses awaken to it.

AWARENESS OF ENVIRONMENT

By observing your baby's development carefully, you will soon see when he is ready to 'play' with an object for, as he grows, he becomes aware of his surroundings, and more conscious of what you are doing, rather than who you are.

Having a mobile for him to look at – particularly a musical one – helps your baby to develop an awareness of objects around him. A simple way of achieving this is to hang little bells by different lengths of ribbon or string above your baby's cot or in front of a window. You can move the bells gently so that they ring quietly while your baby is resting.

RHYTHMIC PLAY

Developing your child's sense of rhythm through music is a wonderful experience for both of you. As he sits on your knee, you can hold a single bell and sing to him, ringing the bell occasionally during the song. Your baby will soon want to hold and rattle the bell himself while you are singing to him. This simple imitation is an amazing impulse.

As your baby grows older and begins to interact with other children, you can 'make music' by shaking bells and rattles while you sing together.

Hints and tips
- Use small flowerpots.
- Use seasoned wood.
- Paint the flowerpots using poster paints and coat with child-safe varnish when finished.
- Make sure the thread is strong and will not break.
- Experiment with different size 'clappers' to produce a range of sounds.
- Do not hang the bells so that they are within easy reach of a small baby.
- An older baby will enjoy playing with just one of these, especially while you sing with him.

'Babies are stimulated into activity through interaction with other human beings.'

Rose Barocio, 'The Role of Warmth, Speech and Attention in Infant Care'

Making *flowerpot bells*

You can use a number of these tiny flowerpot bells to make a mobile, or just use them individually to dangle from your fingers and delight your baby.

How to do it

1 Paint the flowerpots with a design of your choice, leave to dry, then varnish.

2 Decide how long you want the mobile strings to be and cut an appropriate length of strong thread for each flowerpot.

3 Secure a ceramic bead to one end of the thread. This will be the clapper. Tie another bead a little further up the thread to allow the clapper to hang freely inside the flowerpot (this bead must be bigger than the hole in the bottom of the flowerpot to prevent it slipping through).

4 Push the opposite end of the thread up through the hole in the bottom of the flowerpot and pull so that the clapper is now inside the pot. Decorate the thread with different sizes of bead. The bead next to the hole must be large enough not to be pulled through.

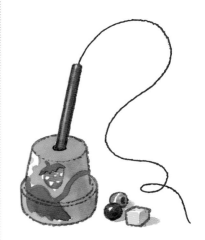

5 Thread the flowerpot strings through the bead holes and tie knots to secure.

6 If you want to make a mobile, arrange the flowerpots on the log slice to determine where they should hang without knocking into one another in a breeze. Mark where the holes for the flowerpot strings and the strings for suspending the mobile will be drilled. For the latter, site two holes close together at each drilling point, so you can feed string down through one hole and back up through the other.

7 Place the slice of log in a vice and drill holes for the flowerpot strings, and also for attaching strings from which to suspend the mobile. If you want to remove the bark completely, strip it off with a power sander. Alternatively, remove any loose bits of bark with sandpaper. Oil and polish with a cloth.

8 Now attach the strings for suspending the mobile, making sure they are long enough to give the required drop. Thread through the flowerpot strings and secure the ends with beads and knots.

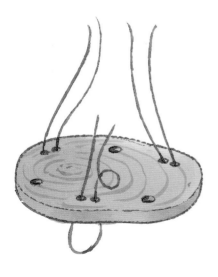

Action

Action

Although no two children are the same, a similar pattern of child development can be found the world over. By observing changes in a child's movements and gestures we gain an insight into inner changes, which we can then interpret and respond to accordingly.

Early activity

For the first year of life your baby is a creature of hand and mouth, getting to know the world more through these than through the eyes. The mouth takes precedence during the first few months, then the hand, and only by the end of the first year do the eyes begin to play a significant role. The process involves both a sensual distancing and a growing awareness of self: first a baby needs to taste the world with her lips and tongue and then touch and move her arms and hands about before she can observe, direct her gaze and point to things. Although your child's eyes and ears are open to the world from birth, she does not use them directly to investigate it until she has them under control.

The hands themselves are subjected to the same oral investigation: fingers, fists and thumbs are run across the mouth and sucked. Your child needs to have tasted her hands before she can properly use them, at around four to five months of age, when she can begin successfully to reach for an object. When she progresses to her hands the primary movement is one of grasping and this too has stages of refinement in the manipulation of fingers and thumb: at three months the crossing of the eye axis occurs and, with it, the ability to focus and so finger play starts; at four months a baby can grasp an object with both hands and bent fingers;

at six months she can grasp things with one hand; at seven months she can hold an object between the thumb and forefinger; and at nine months between the tips of the thumb and forefinger. By 18 months this skill has usually entirely replaced the oral pathway.

Discovering her world

A child's eyes become directed from eight months onwards, until which time they are basically used to localize things. They can then focus on an object, and at this point a child's gaze is intensive and searching. During the second year it will become less so, as things are now more familiar.

A baby has to discover her own body first and, when she has inhabited it to her satisfaction, she can use that body to discover the world around her. She does this by refining her senses and becoming more conscious of movement. This has implications for the toys that you give her. They need to have a certain pliability for her fingers to manipulate them, and they need to stimulate your child's senses so that she reaches about herself with confidence. The first two years of children's lives are universal in character: boys are just as happy playing with dolls as girls are – the importance lies in a baby being able to find her- or himself through play. Only

Making wooden fences

You can make these fences in a range of different sizes, varying the number of bars or posts. Make a five-bar gate, for example, or one with a cross strut.

How to do it

You will need

Seasoned branches

Saw

Sandpaper

Chisel

Flat wooden sticks

PVA glue or hammer and thin panel pins

Boiled linseed oil or olive oil and cloths (optional)

1 For each two-post fence, use a saw to cut two 25 mm (1 in) diameter tree branches in 10 cm (4 in) lengths.

2 Use sandpaper or the side of a chisel to remove any loose bark. Always push the chisel away from you.

3 Sand and trim the ends of the logs to make sure they stand up.

4 Use flat wooden sticks to create the bars, gluing them on to the logs using PVA glue and/or hammering thin panel pins though them. If liked, finish cut surfaces with oil, polishing well with a cloth.

Making wooden blocks

For children over the age of one, you can leave bark on these blocks, but make sure that you sand or chisel off any rough or loose bits.

You will need

Seasoned branches

Vice

Saw

Sandpaper

Chisel

Power sander (if removing all bark)

Boiled linseed oil or olive oil and cloths (optional)

How to do it

1 Place a seasoned branch in a vice and cut a number of discs and cylinders, ranging in diameter from about 2.5–12 cm (1–5 in) and in height from approximately 1.5–12 cm (¾ in–5 in). You will need a good variety of different sizes so that the blocks can be stacked on top of each other.

2 Use sandpaper or the side of a chisel to remove any loose bark. Always push the chisel away from you.

3 Sand and trim the ends of the logs to make sure they stand up.

4 If you want to remove the bark entirely, put the block in a vice and use a power sander to sand it perfectly smooth.

5 If liked, coat sanded sections with oil and polish with a cloth.

Pompoms

A pompom is relaxing for you to make. It is something you can pick up and put down readily, and requires no concentration. Weaving the yarn in and out has a lovely repetitive feel to it and is something that can easily be done while singing your baby to sleep, for example. The repetitive action is soothing and calming for both of you.

SENSORY DELIGHTS

A pompom is most suitable for a baby when she begins to crawl or toddle. Very young babies put everything they touch into their mouths, and a pompom may begin to come apart unless very firmly tied during the making. One idea is to hang a number of firmly made pompoms from a string tied across the cot for the little baby to reach up to and bat to and fro.

Pompoms are soft and fluffy. Squeezing and cuddling them provides a wonderful sensory experience for any older baby. If you hang a pompom from a short string she will have endless fun feeling and pushing it. The sensitivity your baby develops from touching or playing with these pompoms also helps to enliven her sense of touch.

VERSATILE TOYS

Pompoms are very quick and simple to make. You could easily make two in different sizes, one for the head and one for the body, and then combine them to create a wide range of different toys, such as the chick on page 46.

Hints and tips

- Use thick knitting yarn or lengths of carded wool.
- Use firm cardboard for the rings so that they do not bend.
- Cut the hole so that it is big enough to thread the yarn through.
- When making pompoms, be sure to use yarn that does not shed fibres.

'The beginnings of creativity emerge in the way that very young babies see themselves as the cause of making things happen.'

Tina Bruce, *Cultivating Creativity in Babies, Toddlers and Young Children*

Making a pompom

Pompoms are incredibly versatile and can be joined together or sculpted to make all manner of fun soft toys. A single pompom on a short string is fun for a baby to bat.

How to do it

You will need

Sheet of card

Compass

Pencil

Sharp scissors

Yarn

Needle (optional)

1 Use a compass and pencil to make two circles out of card. They must both be the same size.

2 Draw a smaller circle in the centre of each. Again, they must be the same size – about half the radius of the larger circle.

3 Cut out the large circles and then the small ones, to give you two identical rings of card.

4 Put the rings together and start to wind yarn around them tightly and evenly, using a needle if desired. Keep going until you have filled in the hole.

5 Using sharp scissors, begin to cut the yarn along the circumference of the ring – the idea is to cut between the two pieces of card.

6 Take a length of yarn and put it in between the two card rings. Wind it around the centre a couple of times, pull tightly and tie in a knot. Attach a length of yarn for hanging, if desired.

7 Cut away the card, which can now be discarded.

8 Fluff up the pompom and trim any protruding ends if necessary.

Wooden boat

Playing with water is a joy for most children, and babies love nothing more than to splash and float. As babies grow and are able to sit up in the bath, they want toys to play with. Your baby won't be frustrated if the toys roll over or even upside down in the water, but will enjoy pushing them and watching them float away. Your role will be to push them back again!

FLOATING TOY

Constructing a boat from a piece of wood, which floats naturally, is an easy way of making a floating toy. Keep your design simple – young babies don't need sails on the boat until they knows what a sailboat is (watching boats on a river, or taking your child for a row, will communicate the idea). You can vary your design, sometimes keeping the bark on (so long as any loose flakes have been removed), for example, or making the boat wide enough to take little people.

Making the boat from a piece of bark is a creative and imaginative activity: looking for the right shapes in nature helps you to develop a sensitive eye for form. Sanding or whittling at a piece of wood in front of your baby is a rhythmic activity that he loves to watch. Feeling the rough sandpaper and the smooth wood also helps him to develop in a sensory way.

PLAYING WITH THE BOAT

When your baby is more mobile and can play on the floor, create lakes and rivers using blue cloths and make sails out of feathers, fabric or paper. Your baby will enjoy filling boats with little people, animals or even shells and flowers. Animals can also come down to the edge of the lake to drink and watch the boats, and the ducks can float on the river, too. If playing outside, you can float the boat on a puddle, or make a little stream in the garden or in a sandpit.

Move the water gently as you play, allowing the baby to feel its movement and see how the boat can move in different ways. Try singing quietly and rhythmically at the same time. Children love this simple song and yours will enjoy your repeating it over and over again:

'Row, row, row the boat
Gently down the stream
Merrily, merrily, merrily, merrily
Life is but a dream.'

Hints and tips
- Use seasoned wood.
- Make sure loose pieces of bark are removed.
- Boats are best suited to older babies, as they require skill to stay upright.
- Add little people or objects to the boat during play so that you can make up a story.
- Always watch your baby carefully when you are playing with water.

Making a wooden boat

This simple boat design makes a great bath-time toy. You can simplify it for very young babies by removing the mast and sail to leave just the basic boat shape.

How to do it

You will need

Paper

Pencil

Slice of seasoned log, without bark

Vice

Jigsaw

Drill and drill bits

Thin dowelling

Saw

PVA glue

Single-colour felt

Boiled linseed oil or olive oil and cloths

1 Create a simple template by folding a piece of paper in half, drawing a half-boat base shape, cutting it out and unfolding it. Follow the template to draw the boat base shape on the slice of wood (approximately 25 mm/1 in thick) and mark the position of the mast along the horizontal axis.

2 Place the slice of log in a vice and cut out the boat outline using a jigsaw. With the boat base still in the vice, drill the hole for the mast, making sure not to drill right through the wood. Use a drill bit that corresponds to the size of the dowelling.

3 Use a piece of thin dowelling for the mast, sawing it to the desired length and gluing it in position.

4 Cut a triangle of felt, fold it in half and wrap it around the mast. Glue in place, trimming the felt if necessary and gluing to seal the open edge. To protect the wood, oil and polish it with a cloth.

Wooden train

A basic push-along toy, like this train made from segments of seasoned wood, is an ideal plaything for a newly mobile baby and will encourage activity and external movement. Rhythm is particularly important in a child's development. By repeating an exercise, she will discover new movements, build up new skills and strengthen her muscles.

GOING FOR A RIDE

Making this wooden train for your baby requires little skill. In the beginning you can just use a simply formed piece of wood with rounded edges, and flatten the base so that it sits comfortably on the floor. One piece of wood can become a carriage; a number of them can be a train.

The project offers scope for creativity. Carving hollows in the wooden pieces creates seats. You can make an engine piece, for the front of the train, by slicing off the top half of one carriage and carving a pointed nose. You could even screw in a funnel made from a smaller piece of log or construct a cabin for the driver. Knotted squares of fabric can become people to ride in the train.

When your baby is older, you can develop the train further by attaching a screw-in hook to the front face of each carriage, and a screw-in ring to the rear face of each carriage. Your child will then be able to interlink the carriages during play.

FLOOR PLAY

Placing the carriages on a cloth on the floor and building a simple scene around them adds to the fun. A crawling baby will happily play with this, placing little people or animals in and out of the bucket seats, particularly if you join in. If you play with integrity, so that it is real to you too, your baby will absorb your approach and imitate your actions. This will influence her development. Furthermore your baby will enjoy playing with something you have made because it carries with it the effort you have put into the making of it.

Hints and tips

- Use seasoned branches and logs.
- If your baby is 12 months or older, you can leave bark on the train, but remove any loose pieces.
- Sand all sawn parts well and finish with oil.
- Be creative but keep it simple; hooks and rings that require linking are best kept for toddlers.
- Flatten the base so that the carriages of the train do not rock.

'Play is practice for life.'

Sally Jenkinson, *The Genius of Play*

Making a wooden train

If making the toy for a very small baby, sand off the bark completely to prevent baby chewing it off.

How to do it

1 To make the front of the train, place a length of wood in a vice and saw in half lengthways. Cut one end to give it a roughly triangular shape. Still in the vice, use a chisel to gouge out a seat for the driver.

2 To make a carriage, hold a length of wood in a vice and use a chisel to gouge out a seat for a passenger to sit in.

3 Turn the length of wood over and plane off the bottom of the engine or carriage so that it sits flat and does not rock.

4 Repeat Steps 2 and 3 to make a number of carriages and then sand all sawn areas, using a power sander or sandpaper, until they are perfectly smooth.

5 If desired, you can embellish the basic design, perhaps by gluing a smaller log section on to the engine piece, to serve as a funnel.

6 Apply some oil with a cloth to the sanded areas and polish well.

Wheeled car

Children love nothing better than to roll something around. A simple rolling toy, such as a rounded log with wheels, is one that allows your baby the possibility of movement and also stimulates other senses in a gentle way. This project is a version of the basic vehicle idea on page 92, with wheels fixed carefully through the cut log to create a rolling car.

SENSE STIMULATION

This wheeled car is appropriate for different stages of your baby's development. It encourages not only mobility, but also other senses such as hearing. Rolling a push-along toy on a bare floor creates a sound, which is varied when the toy is rolled backwards and forwards. This attracts the attention of a sitting baby, so that he grasps the toy in his hands and begins to play with it. As your baby begins to crawl, he will push and follow such a toy around the room. Soon he will grasp it in his hands, rolling it one-handed, as he crawls.

A wheeled car can be made very easily using a section of log and log slices for wheels, so long as you attach the wheels securely and remember to remove as much bark as possible (or your baby may try to eat it!). Take particular care to remove the bark from the wheels.

Hints and tips

- Use seasoned branches and logs.
- Fix wheels on to dowels extremely well.
- You can leave bark on the car, but try to remove it from wheels unless it is smooth.
- Sand all sawn parts well and finish with oil.
- Make the car small enough for your baby to grasp with ease.

GO FOR A SPIN

Your baby will enjoy moving a driver in and out of the car and taking the car for a drive. You can make a simple figure by gluing a wooden bead to a thin section of log or use a small toy your child already owns. Roll the car to your baby gently. When he is more mobile, you can build a road with ramps made from cushions for him to roll the car down.

'A young child's earliest play involves movement for the pure joy of it.'

Rahima Baldwin Dancy, *You are Your Child's First Teacher*

Making a wheeled car

As well as scooping out seats for the driver and passengers, you can drill some way into each length of wood, to make a hole big enough to take a wooden figure.

How to do it

You will need

Seasoned logs

Chisel

Sandpaper

Vice

Drill and drill bits

Saw

Thin dowelling

PVA glue

Boiled linseed oil or olive oil and cloths

I Select a length of log for the body of the car. Use the side of a chisel to scrape off any loose bark from the side, always pushing the chisel away from you. Sand the log smooth.

2 With the log held in a vice, use a chisel to cut out a scallop, which will be the seat for the car's driver.

3 If you are making a wooden figure from a thin segment of log or are planning to use a particular toy, drill a hole to accommodate the base of the driver while the log is still in the vice. Do not drill right through the car.

4 Still holding the log in a vice, drill straight through the log from side to side to create a hole for the dowel that will hold the front wheels. Repeat for the back wheels. Use a drill bit that corresponds to your dowel size.

5 Take the car out of the vice. Trim two lengths of dowelling to size, allowing enough to go through the body of the car and hold the wheels on either side. Feed the dowels through the two drilled holes.

Cut four same-size log slices for wheels
and sand smooth. Drill a hole in each centre
for the dowel (do not drill right through).

Glue a wheel firmly to each end of the
dowel. Finish by coating all cut surfaces with
oil and polishing with a cloth.

Wheeled car 97

Push-along toy

Toys with wheels offer endless possibilities for play. When your baby becomes more mobile, a push-along toy is the ideal plaything for stimulating external movement as she learns to crawl and then toddle. It will keep her mobile and encourage movement, which is crucial in the first years of development. Repetitive movement is an aid to learning and discovery, strengthening the physical body and teaching control.

VERSATILE DESIGN

In addition to keeping your child mobile and encouraging movement and balance, a push-along toy will stimulate her capacity for play and may even increase her ability to interact with others. A natural progression from the simple wheeled car described on page 96 is a larger toy that is suitable for the crawler, the toddler and the walker. The same design can be used for all ages, but the length of the handle and shape of the wheels should be adapted, according to the age of your baby and the different ways in which she will play with it.

Hints and tips
- Use seasoned wood.
- Remove all bark from the handle and wheels.
- Be inventive: your toy can take on any shape that appeals to your child – horse or pig, car or tractor – and can be made larger, if preferred.
- Measure the length of the handle to suit the height of your child.
- Make sure you add a rounded tip to the handle.

If you simply add wheels to the basic animal shape, a crawling baby can push it around. She will take delight in making it move by herself and in the fact that it will roll away from her with a little push. Crawling after the toy is great fun, too. If you roll the toy between you and your baby, remember to turn it so it always rolls head first.

The next stage is to add an animal tail as a handle for your child to hold on to. This handle can be different lengths. As soon as she is walking, you can make her a toy with a handle that is long enough to push the toy in front of her as she walks.

For all models, make sure that the wheels are not too large, and that your baby can easily hold on to the handle end of the toy. If you off set the wheels – that is, if you drill the holes just off-centre – the push-along toy will bounce along the ground as it moves, much to your baby's delight.

DIFFERENT STAGES

As parents, we need to be aware of our baby's individual progression and what is suitable for her particular stage of development, not her age. If you give a baby a toy that she is not yet ready for she may become frustrated. Don't be upset if this happens, but put the toy away for a while and bring it out later.

Making a push-along toy

You could change the design of this toy to reflect your baby's favourite animal – a chick or a penguin, for example. Offsetting the wheels gives the toy a comical bounce.

How to do it

1 Draw a duck design on paper in pencil, trace it and transfer it to a slice of wood, approximately 25 mm (1 in) thick. Transfer the tracing by flipping the tracing paper, placing it on the wood and rubbing over it.

2 Place the slice of wood in a vice and cut out your design using a jigsaw. Still in the vice, drill a hole in the duck shape for the thin dowel that will connect the two wheels.

3 Using the same thickness wood, cut two circles for the wheels. Draw them first with a compass to make sure they are both the same size.

4 Drill a hole on each wheel, for the thin dowel. The hole should be slightly off-centre and in the same place on each wheel. To mark the spot for drilling, pencil short lines showing the vertical and horizontal axes running out of the compass pinprick in the centre of each wheel. Align the wheels and lay the length of thin dowelling over them so that the lower edge of the dowelling is aligned with the horizontal axis. Mark a short line on each wheel where the upper side of the dowelling intersects with the vertical axis. Drill between the two horizontal marks, on the vertical line. Do not drill all the way through the wheel.

5 Cut the thin dowelling to length, to make a dowel that will go from one wheel through the body of the duck and into the other wheel.

6 Use a thicker piece of dowelling for the handle and cut it to the desired length, suitable for your child to push the toy while standing up. Return the duck shape to the vice and drill a hole in the end of the tail to accommodate the dowel.

7 Assemble the toy. Thread the thin dowel through the duck and glue a wheel firmly on to each end. Glue the handle into the rear end of the duck and finish the other end of the handle with a large bead.

8 Use a black felt-tipped pen to draw an eye on each side of the duck, if required. Finish by coating the duck with oil and polishing with a cloth.

Action chutes

Babies love things that move or that cause movement. It is wonderful to see the delight an older baby expresses when she first experiences pouring. She loves to watch water trickle or flow from one place to another – it enlivens all her senses. This action chute encourages creativity and adventurousness.

CREATIVE PLAY

Even when your baby is tiny, she will react to your trickling water on her tummy. As she grows and is able to sit, she will gain endless satisfaction from playing with pouring implements in the bath, paddling pool, over the sink or by the stream. These can include little cups, jugs and spoons.

Making something for an older baby to use for pouring games, such as this action chute, enables her to become more creative in her play. If you make the chute narrow, she can pour or trickle dry sand down it. A larger chute will accommodate fleece balls or pompoms (see pages 60 and 82).

Making a series of chutes in different sizes and colours enables your baby to begin to see that things not only slide, but drop. You can lean the chutes against a cushion, balance them on wooden blocks or, if playing in sand, prop them up with forked sticks stuck into the sand. Using different levels allows items to drop from one chute to another, even to change direction. This is rudimentary scientific play!

Hints and tips
- Use brightly coloured, or painted, paper.
- Avoid patterns, which can be distracting.
- Varnish the chutes well to preserve them if they are going to be used with wet sand or water.
- Use thick paper to make sturdy chutes.
- Try covering different sizes and lengths of tubing.
- Always supervise your baby when she is playing with water.

SPIRIT OF ADVENTURE

You can use these chutes for floor play – turn one upside down for a tunnel or balance one on blocks for a bridge. Use a chute as a boat filled with people and animals sailing down a blue-cloth sea; fence the garden or roof the house with them. The limitless possibilities of a toy like this will enable your baby to become adventurous.

'Experimenting with doing the same thing in a different way is an aspect of the creative process.'

Tina Bruce, *Cultivating Creativity in Babies, Toddlers and Young Children*

Making an action chute

You can make a number of these chutes in a variety of colours, using different sized tubes taken from the centres of rolls of kitchen towel or aluminium foil.

How to do it

You will need

Cardboard tubes

Sharp scissors

Painted paper

PVA glue

Child-safe varnish (optional)

1 Use sharp scissors to remove a strip of card down the entire length of the cardboard tube. The strip can be wide or narrow, depending on how wide you wish the chute to be.

2 Cut a piece of painted paper to fit around the inside and the outside of the chute, allowing extra for overlapping on all sides.

3 Glue the paper to the interior of the chute, leaving sufficient on both sides to overlap at the back of the chute. Cut small nicks in the excess paper at the short ends and fold these over the outside of the tube, gluing in place.

4 Take both long sides of the painted paper around the outside of the chute, overlapping them at the back and glue. Trim any loose ends or edges neatly.

5 Repeat Steps 1–4 to make additional chutes of different lengths or widths. If liked, use child-safe varnish to protect the chutes.

Wonder

Wonder

Wonder forms the basis on which respect for ourselves and the world is built. It is our sense of wonder that finds beauty in the world and which revivifies us when faced with distress or calamity. It should therefore be acknowledged as a uniquely human experience that enters deeply into our souls. Without wonder life would be dreary indeed. Our babies bring it with them into our lives and express it through play.

The seeds of wonder

Wonder is a natural response in our early years and needs cultivating throughout childhood as a basis for healthy learning. When a child sees the face of a simple, well-made rag doll with no clearly defined or specified features it leaves him a space into which he can project his own emotion, fantasy and creative energy. This is not to be underestimated, for the child can make the doll laugh, cry, be angry or tired, speak or be silent. Just as sport and music can be practised so, too, can creativity, and babies, toddlers and young children have a natural inclination to be creative.

Such activity contains the seeds of wonder – a much stronger concept than is suggested by the word 'pretend' during play. As a parent of a baby, you yourself will be filled with wonder at this new creation for whom you are now responsible and who will change your life for good. The wonder you feel for your child, who craves and reciprocates your love, creates a spiritual ambience around him, which is absorbed and in turn feeds the child's own respect for others and is a source of confident creativity. Wonder is the basis of science and is a primary emotion out of which investigative and

analytical consciousness can fruitfully flow. Through wonder our imagination is enlivened and we can recreate the world. As Albert Einstein wrote:

'When I examine myself and my methods of thought, I come to the conclusion that the gift of fantasy has meant more to me than any talent for abstract, positive thinking.'

It's a wonderful world

As a parent your task is to create a world around your child in which wonder is undiminished. The toys you make, no matter how simple to adult eyes, are a source of wonder for your child. Watch as he tries to make sense of the colours reflected on his wall from the window decoration (see page 122) or handles each item in his treasure box as if seen for the very first time (see page 114). What adults call the 'reality' of life will intervene soon enough, but allowing the world to be truly wonderful supports your child's ability to develop the necessary faculties for coping with the 'real' world later in life.

It is worth repeating that you are investing a part of yourself when you create toys for your child, and as a consequence you are making them more than just material objects in your child's eyes. It's also important to remember that, when you play with your child, even the words and the tone of voice you use to accompany play will reinforce his

Influential thought

What we think about other humans has an impact on both them and on ourselves, although it is not tangible. Thoughts are not neutral and do not just live privately, as it were, within our brains. As the Soviet developmental psychologist, Lev Vygotsky, pointed out, every thought contains a transmuted element of feeling. Loving thoughts are a reality and a baby thrives on them. How we involve ourselves in play transmits more than we imagine, as love is reciprocal, and we can find sustenance in a baby's love and trust in us.

imaginative response to the toy, because language has its wonders, too.

The moment when your baby smiles at you and you smile back is also a wonder for your child, as he wakes up to the potential of human relationships. He becomes aware that a world of feelings exists beyond himself and that he can have an effect on it.

Forging a spiritual bond

Wonder is at the core of spirituality, a much used but vague word that signifies our humanity. Spirituality is not necessarily only to be found in complex processes of inner training, bodily denial or profound existential thought, but can exist among the simple things of life. Our love for, and wonder of, a child are a spiritual experience that goes beyond subconscious survival mechanisms, genetic inheritance and the instinct to protect the next generation. Our children bring us directly into contact, sometimes in a startling way, with the wonder that may have receded from our lives.

Creative play in its manifold contexts and appearances is a revealing and timeless spiritual process. Arguably, contemporary life needs it even more as a therapeutic antidote to what we have made of our modern world. Blake's 'grain of sand' imagery, in his poem 'Auguries of Innocence', is a contemplation of early childhood. Fortunately, our children can remind us of it and lead us there if we are prepared to open ourselves to its beauty:

> 'To see a World in a Grain of Sand
> And a Heaven in a Wild Flower,
> Hold Infinity in the palm of your hand
> And Eternity in an hour.'

This view is not another-worldly or a sentimental approach to life but a realistic interpretation of who we and who our children are. Consider this as you make toys for, and play with, your baby and you are sure to find a dimension of wonder from which you and your family will benefit.

Sand box

Children have a special relationship with nature and it is important for them to be outside for much of the time, but this may not always be possible. A portable sand box is a way of enabling your children to play outside – and of bringing the outside in when going out is not an option.

IMAGINATIVE PLAY

Sand is a most wonderful plaything, to which you can add water for easy moulding or leave dry for pouring and trickling. You can make more than one box, filling each with something different – sand or mud, water or conkers. Your baby will learn from you that the mud belongs in the mud box, the sand in the sand box, and so on. Mud, earth and sand are a child's first modelling clay. She can squeeze or squish them and mould them into anything she wants, making towers, castles and roads – the possibilities for imaginative play are endless. She will love building tunnels with you if your fingers appear at the other end!

If you choose to introduce implements, keep them simple: a large shell makes a great spade and is just the right size for little hands. Sieves or colanders and little cups or jugs are also useful. As your baby grows, include some pretty shells and stones of different shapes for making patterns and designs in the sand.

A sandpit provides a great opportunity for cooperative play; to share and build something with a friend. Your baby may find enough to do on her own and if a friend joins her, will happily play alongside, sharing the occasional sand toy.

Hints and tips

- If making the box yourself, use sturdy planks of seasoned wood. Screw them together and use wood glue for the joints.
- Make sure the handles are strong as the box is heavy when filled with sand.
- Use proper play sand and do not overfill the box.
- Line the box with polythene to keep the sand in good condition and protect it from pests.
- Keep any toys in a separate box.
- Drill holes in the base to allow water to drain out.
- Make a cover, particularly if using outside.

'Very young children are moved to play, experiment with and rearrange the materials of their world.'

Margaret Morgan, *Natural Childhood*

Making a sand box

An old wine crate works well for this project – ask your local wine merchant for one. Alternatively make a wooden box with a solid bottom from planks of seasoned wood, finishing it with oil.

How to do it

You will need

- Wooden box or crate with solid bottom
- Tape measure
- Pencil
- Drill and drill bit
- Length of rope
- Polythene sheeting
- Brown packaging tape
- Staple gun
- Wooden beading
- Saw
- PVA glue
- Screwdriver and short screws

1 Find the centre of each short side of the wooden box (marking in pencil so that it can be rubbed out afterwards) and drill two holes either side, approximately 7–10 cm (3–4 in) apart.

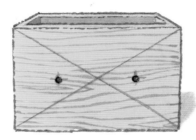

2 Thread a length of rope through the drilled holes, tying a knot in each end of the rope on the inside of the box to create two handles.

3 Use polythene sheeting to line the inside of the box in order to make it watertight. You can use brown tape to seal any overlapping edges.

4 Use a staple gun to secure the polythene to the inside rim of the box.

5 Cover the staples with a length of wooden beading, cut to size and mitred at the ends to fit in the corners. Glue the beading in position and screw to fix.

6 The box is ready for filling with sand.

Treasure basket

This concept originated with educator Elinor Goldschmied, who inspired generations of parents, children and early years workers. It is appropriate for a baby who can sit up, but is not yet very mobile. Putting interesting objects in a basket enables your baby to discover for herself what she can do with them.

IMAGINATIVE PLAY

Providing your baby with a treasure basket keeps her occupied and stimulated for a long period of time. It also allows you to let your child make her own discoveries. As parents we need to learn when not to interfere with our babies' learning, sometimes attending to them only when they need us. Try watching your baby play with the items in the treasure basket, exploring quietly by herself, and only talk to her when she initiates it.

The basket can be quite small and needs to be strong. A drawstring liner is useful for holding the objects safely and, if you are going out and want to take them with you, doubles as a drawstring bag to carry them around.

TREASURES FOR THE BASKET

There is only one rule for choosing objects to go in the basket: they must appeal to your baby's senses. For this reason, natural materials are preferable. Plastic is cold, hard and mostly angular and generally does not appeal to our senses. Natural materials are usually warm to the touch and can be of any shape. A stone can be heavy, flat, rough or smooth and warms up when played with.

Your baby will 'taste' the objects too, so make sure they are suitable for little mouths. Scraping her teeth across a stone is an interesting experience for her. It allows her to absorb the feel of the stone – and does no harm. A pine cone is good as she can hold it comfortably and explore it with interest, perhaps throw it, but make sure the pine seeds have been removed and that the cone is safe with no loose bits. A soup spoon is fun: your child can bang it, eat with it or use it as a mirror. An eggcup, different sized wooden spoons, a rattle, metal tea strainer, shell and silk cloth are all also great treasures for exploration.

Hints and tips
- Line the basket with material that is strong enough to double as a carry bag for the treasures.
- Make more than one basket to use as storage for your baby's toys.
- Use strong baskets; square or rectangular ones tip over less easily than round ones.
- Choose treasures made from natural materials.
- Objects will go in the mouth, so make sure they are a safe size – not too small.
- If including material or a silk scarf, make sure it is square and not long.
- Do not choose too many objects: ten in the basket at a time is plenty.
- Allow your baby enough time to get to know the objects and discover what they can do before you change them.

Making a *treasure basket*

The method described here can be used for any size of rectangular or square basket. Make sure the basket is shallow enough for your baby to reach into easily.

How to do it

You will need

Rectangular or square basket

Fabric

Tape measure

Dressmaking scissors

Needle and thread

Pins

Yarn or ribbon

Safety pin (optional)

1 First cut the fabric pieces. Take your measurements from the basket itself, remembering to add a little extra for seam allowances. You can place the basket on top of your fabric to measure the base.

2 For the sides, you can use one continuous length of fabric. When it comes to measuring the depth, remember to allow for the amount of overhang you want. Always take into account any pattern of the fabric when cutting.

3 Sew the top hem of the fabric for the sides, making it wide enough to thread the yarn or ribbon through later. (See Step 6.)

4 Sew the vertical seam and place the fabric in position on the basket, checking any pattern so that the best side of the fabric faces the front. Pin to mark each corner. Place the fabric for the base inside the basket, right side up and, again, pin to mark the position of each corner.

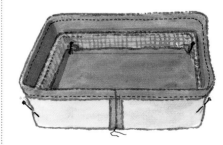

5 Remove the fabrics and sew them together, wrong sides out, using the pin markers to align the corners correctly.

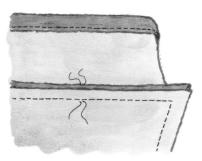

6 Make a small cut in the centre of the long top hem that will be at the front of the basket and feed through a length of yarn or ribbon, tying the ends in a bow to finish. Tying the yarn on to a safety pin will make it easier to feed through the hem. Take care to remove all pins before letting your baby play with the basket.

Nature mobile

In the first few months, your baby's main task is to build his physical strength through development of his muscles. He also needs to recognize and understand his body, and become accustomed to what it is capable of doing. Toys that he can look at while lying in his cot, or when sitting in a highchair, will catch his attention for fleeting moments. He will soon begin to focus on them and want to touch them.

BRINGING NATURE INDOORS

Lifting your baby up to look at the mobile, and moving it gently for him, will give him much joy. As your baby begins to focus on this object outside of the periphery of his own body, his senses will be stimulated by the variety, colour, shape and sound of the objects hanging from the mobile.

There are countless ideas for interesting seasonal natural materials that you can collect and suspend from the mobile: dried leaves, pine cones, conkers and beech nuts in the autumn; feathers, shells, drift wood and flowers in summer. String your chosen items from branches with cord threaded with beads or brass bells and hang the mobile above the cot, or in front of a window to blow gently in the breeze. It is important not to suspend too many things from one mobile. Instead, change the mobile from time to time so that your baby begins to look out for the different shapes and colours of the items you have selected.

As your baby grows, collect items together while you are out on a walk. This will enliven his interest in nature. He will begin to appreciate that a feather comes from a bird and get to know what it feels like to touch, its sleekness and how light it is. He will hold a shell and feel its hard, sometimes sharp edges, and will taste the salt of the sea. He will begin to realize that if pulled, the petals will come off a flower as he holds it.

SEASONAL TOUCH

Other ideas for mobiles include stars and angels for Christmas; hearts and little fleece birds on Valentine's Day; blown and painted eggs at Easter; paper snowflakes and pompom snowballs in winter. You could make the mobile with small fleece balls or corn dollies – the possibilities are endless.

Hints and tips

- Make sure that the collected items do not drop or shed seeds.
- Use strong thread or nylon cord for hanging.
- Make sure the branch from which the items are suspended is strong.
- Hang the branch safely and securely.
- Use a variety of shapes, colours and sounds.

Making a nature mobile

This mobile has an autumnal look to it, but you can easily adapt the idea to suit other seasons, making bees and butterflies for summer, angels and snowflakes for winter, and flowers for spring.

How to do it

You will need

Length of willow

Strong thread

Selection of natural decorations, such as pine cones, feathers, dried leaves and flowers

1 Make a ring from a length of willow, approximately 100 cm (40 in), weaving the willow in and out of the hoop as you go. Tie the hoop at regular intervals with thread, to secure it.

2 Tie three equal-length threads to the willow hoop and knot together at the top. You will use these to suspend the mobile when it is complete.

3 Cut several pieces of different-length thread and tie a selection of natural decorations on to each, leaving a gap between each one and the next.

4 Tie the decorated strings to the willow hoop, equally spaced around the ring.

Window decoration

Creating a beautiful environment for your baby helps to develop his aesthetic sense. A seasonal window decoration, accompanied by a nature table of collected treasures, will enable him to appreciate his surroundings, and the care you give them, as well as the changes in the passing year.

CHANGING SEASONS

The window decoration will attract your child's attention, particularly when he is more mobile and begins to notice what is happening in nature. Drawing his awareness to the changing seasons by altering its content, design and colour will help broaden his knowledge of the outside world. He will take an interest in the way light shines through the decoration and the reflections it casts on walls.

You will find that layering one colour on top of another in the decoration creates a third colour, while layering the same colour on top of itself, gives that colour depth. You can also tear or twist the tissue into shapes and balls to give the decoration texture. An older baby will enjoy making window decorations with you, sticking bits of torn tissue on to tracing paper. Any artistic activity is a creative experience for your baby, whether he participates in it or watches you do it.

You can make different designs throughout the year. For example, add leaves to a recognizable tree design of trunk and branches, changing their colour according to the seasons. Blossoms can appear on the tree in spring, birds in summer, apples in autumn and stars or snow in winter.

NATURE TABLE

The window decoration can be complemented with a seasonal nature table that can be placed in a convenient place, such as on a window sill or small table. When you are out for a walk, exclaim over your discoveries with your baby, then bring them home to add to the table. A baby takes pleasure in the simplest things – feeling the difference between a sharp stone and a smooth pebble or smelling the scent of mint or rose. Bringing the wonder of nature into your home will be a joy for all of you, awakening the family's interest in nature and the change of the seasons.

Hints and tips

- Cut the decoration frame to any shape, but round the corners as this is more pleasing to the eye.
- Choose a frame colour that suits the transparency.
- Make your design as simple or complicated as you wish, experimenting just with colours to begin with.
- Change the window decoration seasonally.
- If your child is helping, use safe glue.
- Hang the decoration against the window glass.
- For the nature table, use seasonal items – leaves, cones, flowers, berries – or other natural items, such as stones and feathers, and keep it simple.
- Do not let greenery and flowers wilt.
- Choose objects that your baby will not choke on.

Making a window decoration

You can use this technique to make a window decoration for any season of the year: a sunflower for summer, a snowman for winter, blossom for spring and a tree with a squirrel for autumn.

You will need

Two sheets of coloured card

Compass

Pencil

Sharp scissors

Tracing paper

PVA glue

Coloured tissue paper

Hole punch

Coloured string

Decorations for the nature table, such as fresh or dried flowers, non-poisonous berries, twigs, cones, stones, shells, soft cloths in natural colours

How to do it

1 Use a compass to draw a large circle, measuring approximately 30 cm (12 in), on a sheet of card.

2 Draw a second circle approximately 4 cm (1½ in) inside the first and cut out, leaving you with a large card ring. Repeat Steps 1 and 2 for the second sheet of card.

3 Sandwich a sheet of tracing paper between the two card rings and glue it in place along the inside of the rings. Allow the glue to dry.

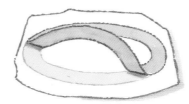

4 Draw a simple seasonal design on to the tracing paper – this project uses a sunflower design for summer.

5 Gradually glue on torn or scrunched-up tissue paper or dried flowers and pressed leaves to create the design. Leave the decoration to dry thoroughly.

6 Cut around the circumference of the card frame, make a hole at the top using a hole punch and tie on a piece of coloured string for hanging up the decoration.

7 Create a nature table to accompany the window decoration. Choose a site that your baby can reach and arrange a selection of safe, natural items on a background cloth.

Index

A
abuse, physical 52
accelerated learning 10
action 74–7
action chutes 102–5
animals 17
 fences for 78
 knitted sheep 42–5
 push-along toys 98–101
 soft hen 38–41
anxiety 14
attention span 17
awareness 52–5

B
balance, building blocks 78
balls
 ball games 60
 fleece 60–3
 pompoms 82–5
Barocio, Rose 68
basket, treasure 114–17
bells, flowerpot 68–71
birds
 pompom chick 46–9
 push-along toy 98–101
 soft hen 38–41
Blake, William 6, 9, 109
blocks and fences 78–81
boat, wooden 86–9
boxes, shakers 56–7, 59
boys, gender differences
 74–6
brain development 10, 14
Britz-Crecelius, Heidi 18
Bruce, Tina 82, 102
Buber, Martin 52
building blocks 78–81

C
car, wheeled 94–7
care 14–17
chick, pompom 46–9
Christmas 118
chutes, action 102–5
colours 54, 122
crawling 82
creative play 102, 108, 109
cuddly doll 21–5

D
Dancy, Rahima Baldwin 94
doll's hammock 34–7
dolls
 and creativity 108
 cuddly doll 21–5
 gender differences 74–6
 floor puppets 26–9
 play development 76
 role play 17
 simple doll 18–20
duck, push-along 98–101

E
ears, hearing 6, 54
Easter 118
Einstein, Albert 108
emotions
 balancing 14
 deprivation 14
 emotional awareness 55
 wonder and 109
expressions, facial 16, 17
eyesight 54, 74

F
fabric projects
 cuddly doll 21–5
 doll's hammock 34–7
 floor puppets 26–9
 simple doll 18–20
 soft hen 38–41
 wall hanging 30–3
facial expressions 16, 17
families, farm animals
 38, 42
fantasy play 76
farm animals
 fences for 78
 knitted sheep 42–5
 pompom chick 46–9
 soft hen 38–41
fear 14
feelings see emotions
fences 78–9, 81
finger play 74
fleece balls 60–3
floor puppets 26–9
floor scenes

action chutes 102
farms 42
fences 78
 with floor puppets 26
 wooden train 90
flowerpot bells 68–71
Froebel, Friedrich 61, 75
functional play 76

G
games, ball 60
'gazelle boy' 76
gender differences 74–6
gestures 54, 77
girls, gender differences
 74–6
Goldschmied, Elinor 114
grasping 74, 76

H
hammock, doll's 34–7
hand control 74, 77
hearing 6, 54
hen, soft 38–41
Hobson, Peter 55

I
imaginative play
 development of 76
 sand box 110
 treasure basket 114
 wonder and 108
imitation 16
 learning to walk 76
 speech development 77

J
Jaffke, Freya 21, 46
Jenkinson, Sally 90

K
'kid-pushing' 10
knitted sheep 42–5
knotted dolls 18–20

L
language development
 76–7
Largo, Dr Remo 76

love, importance of 14
lullabies 34

M
memories 76
mental-health problems 14
mobiles
 flowerpot bells 68–71
 nature mobile 118–21
 wind chime 64–7
Morgan, Margaret 110
motor skills 78
mouth, sense of taste
 54, 74
movement
 development of 56
 and development of
thought 76
 and self-awareness 54
 walking 76
music
 flowerpot bells 68–71
 wind chime 64–7
 see also singing

N
natural materials 114
nature mobile 118–21
nature table 122, 124–5
noises, loud 64
nursery rhymes
 about sheep 42
 ball games 60
 lullabies 34
 water play 86
nurturing instincts 17

P
parenting, joy of 9
physical abuse 52
Pikler, Emmi 18
play
 definition 7–8
 development of 76
 importance of 16–17
 parent's role 17
pompoms 82–5
 pompom chick 46–9
posture, upright 76

pouring games 102
primary senses 52–4
puppets 17
    floor puppets 26–9
push-along toys
    duck 98–101
    wheeled car 94–7
    wooden train 90–3

R
rattles 56–8
reacting to your baby 6–7,
    9–10
reflex movements 56
repetition 17, 56, 77
representative play 76
rhythms 68, 77
rocking 34
role-play 17
    with floor puppets 26
rolling toys, wheeled car
    94–7

S
safety 54
sand
    action chutes 102
    sand box 110–13
seasons, window
    decoration 122
security 14–16
self-awareness
    developing 55
    movement and 54
    and sense development
    52
self-esteem 17
senses, development of
    52–4
sequential play 76
shakers 56–7, 59
sheep, knitted 42–5
sight 54, 74
simple doll 18–20
singing
    and speech development
    77
    'tidying up' song 30
smell, sense of 54

smiling 109
soft hen 38–41
songs see singing
sounds 54
    flowerpot bells 68–71
    wind chime 64–7
speech development 76–7
spirituality 109
Steiner, Rudolf 10–11,
    16, 64
Steiner Waldorf education
    10–11
story-telling 54, 77
stress 14, 55
symbolical play 76

T
talking 76–7
taste, sense of 54, 74
textures 56
thought
    development of 55
    feeling and 109
    movement and
development of 76
tidying up 30
time, sense of 76
tissue, window decoration
    122–4
touch, sense of 52–4, 74
train, wooden 90–3
treasure basket 114–17

V
Valentine's Day 118
vision 54, 74
Vygotsky, Lev 109

W
walking 76
wall hanging 30–3
water play
    pouring games 102
    wooden boat 86–9
wheeled car 94–7
wind chime 64–7
window decoration 122–4
'wolf children' 76
wonder 108–9

wood
    blocks and fences 78–81
    push-along toy 98–101
    rattles 56–8
    wheeled car 94–7
    wind chime 64–7
    wooden boat 86–9
    wooden train 90–3
wool
    fleece balls 60–3
    knitted sheep 42–5
    pompom chick 46–9
    pompoms 82–5

Further reading

Baldwin Dancy, Rahima, *You are Your Child's First Teacher*, Hawthorn Press, Stroud, 2006

Barocio, Rose, 'The Role of Warmth, Speech and Attention in Infant Care', in Michaela Glöckler (ed.), *The Dignity of the Young Child: Care and Training for the First Three Years of Life*, Medical Section of the Goetheanum, Dornach, 1999

Blake, William, *Selected Poetry*, Oxford University Press, Oxford, 1998

Britz-Crecelius, Heidi, *Children at Play: Using Waldorf Principles to Foster Childhood Development*, Inner Traditions, Rochester, 1996

Bruce, Tina, *Cultivating Creativity in Babies, Toddlers and Young Children*, Hodder Arnold, London, 2004

Buber, Martin, *I and Thou*, Continuum International Publishing Group, London and New York, 2004

Carey, Diana and Large, Judy, *Festivals, Family and Food*, Hawthorn Press, Stroud, 2001

Clouder, Christopher and Rawson, Martyn, *Waldorf Education: Rudolf Steiner's Ideas in Practice*, Floris Books, Edinburgh, 2003

Clouder, Christopher (ed.), *Steiner Education: An Introductory Reader*, Sophia Books, Oakland, 2004

Clouder, Christopher, Jenkinson, Sally and Large, Martin (eds.), *The Future of Childhood*, Hawthorn Press, Stroud, 2000

Cohen, David, *The Development of Play*, Routledge, Abingdon, 2006

Druitt, Ann, Fynes-Clinton, Christine and Rowling, Marye, *All Year Round*, Hawthorn Press, Stroud, 1995

Froebel, Friedrich, *The Education of Man*, Dover Publications, Mineola, 2005

Froebel, Friedrich, *The Pedagogics of the Kindergarten: Ideas Concerning the Play and Playthings of the Child*, University Press of the Pacific, Honolulu, 2003

Gerhardt, Sue, *Why Love Matters: How Affection Shapes a Baby's Brain*, Brunner-Routledge, London, 2004

Glöckler, Michaela and Goebel, Wolfgang, *A Guide to Child Health*, Floris Books, Edinburgh, 2003

Glöckler, Michaela (ed.), *The Dignity of the Young Child: Care and Training for the First Three Years of Life*, Medical Section of the Goetheanum, Dornach, 1999

Hobson, Peter, The *Cradle of Thought: Exploring the Origins of Thinking*, Pan Macmillan, London, 2004

Jaffke, Freya, *Play and Work in Early Childhood*, Floris Books, Edinburgh, 2002

Jaffke, Freya, *Toymaking with Children*, Floris Books, Edinburgh, 2003

Jenkinson, Sally, *The Genius of Play: Celebrating the Spirit of Childhood*, Hawthorn Press, Stroud, 2002

Knabe, Angelika, 'Rhythms in Man and Cosmos: Strengthening the Will and Self Assurance' in Michaela Glöckler (ed.), *The Dignity of the Young Child: Care and Training for the First Three Years of Life*, Medical Section of the Goetheanum, Dornach, 1999

Largo, H. Remo, *Babyjahre*, Piper, Munich, 2000

Male, Dot, *The Parent and Child Group Handbook: A Steiner/Waldorf Approach*, Hawthorn Press, Stroud, 2006

Morgan, Margaret, *Natural Childhood*, Gaia Books, London, 1994

Oldfield, Lynne, *Free to Learn: Introducing Steiner Waldorf Early Childhood Education*, Hawthorn Press, Stroud, 2001

Olfman, Sharna (ed.), *All Work and No Play: How Education Reforms are Harming Our Preschoolers*, Praeger, Westport, 2003

Salter, Joan, *The Incarnating Child*, Hawthorn Press, Stroud, 1992

Steiner, Rudolf, *The Education of the Child: And Early Lectures on Education*, Steiner Books, Great Barrington, 1996

Stern, Daniel, *Diary of a Baby: What Your Child Sees, Feels and Experiences*, Basic Books, New York, 1992

Woodhead, Martin, Faulkner, Dorothy and Littleton, Karen (eds.), *Cultural Worlds of Early Childhood*, Routledge, London, 1998

Find out more about the Alliance for Childhood at http://www.allianceforchildhood.org.uk.

Acknowledgements

Author acknowledgements
The authors would like to thank all those who helped in producing this book, either with their explicit support or implicit inspiration. This also applies to our respective children – Leoma and Kether and Emma and Alexandra – who taught us so much before they knew they were doing so.

Photographic acknowledgements
Special Photography © Octopus Publishing Group Limited/Russell Sadur

Publisher acknowledgements
The publisher would like to thank Fiona White for making all the toys in this book. Thanks also to all the children who were photographed for the book (and their parents and guardians for bringing them along): Amelia Thorpe, Angel Baxter, Bethan Steel, Dylan Rees-Coshan, Emma Craig, Imogen Jackson, Ivy Rostron, Jake Franklin, Jamie Clark, Jaya Morrison, Jemma Jessup, Joey Wren, Joseph Coury Reid, Lola Beer, Lydia Cully, Madeline Hesketh, Millie Austin

Executive editors Jo Godfrey Wood and Jessica Cowie
Editor Fiona Robertson
Executive art editor Leigh Jones
Designer Peter Gerrrish
Illustrator Kate Simunek
Production controller Simone Nauerth
Toymaker Fiona White